CANADA

AN HISTORICAL MAGAZINE

Editor: David P. Gagan   Associate Editor: Brian McCutcheon

VOLUME I   NUMBER I   AUTUMN 1973

Published Quarterly by Holt, Rinehart and Winston of Canada,
Limited in Association with McMaster University

Reviews

The editors invite the submission of manuscripts suitable for publication in *Canada*. Manuscripts should be submitted in duplicate accompanied by a stamped, self-addressed envelope. Length of articles should be appropriate to the subject, but generally articles should not exceed 7000 words in length, nor be shorter than 3000 words. All direct quotations should be referenced and, in addition, the editors require an explanatory note on the sources from which articles are written. Articles published in *Canada* are paid for at the rate of $10.00 per printed page on publication. Manuscripts should be sent c/o the Editor, *Canada*, Department of History, McMaster University, Hamilton, Ontario.

Canada: An Historical Magazine is published quarterly by Holt, Rinehart and Winston of Canada, Limited, 55 Horner Avenue, Toronto, Ontario M8Z 4X6, in association with McMaster University, Hamilton, Ontario.

Subscription Rates:

Institutions $14/year
Personal Subscription . . . . $ 9/year
(Personal subscription must be accompanied by payment)

Copyright © 1973 by Holt, Rinehart and Winston of Canada, Limited

ISBN 0-03-927900-6

Cover illustration:
Detail from the Carte de Vallard of 1546
Reproduced by permission of
The Huntington Library, San Marino, California

A Letter from the Editor

What is *CANADA*? It is not a journal of opinion, nor is it an academic quarterly in which professionals write for each other. *CANADA* is a magazine for people who enjoy history — broadly defined — served up in a highly readable, visually appealing medium but nevertheless history which instructs as well as delights. Our goal is to reach and to serve that broad, informed, but not necessarily professional audience of Canadians who regularly read Canadian history as part of their literary diet.

Each of our forthcoming issues will contain up to half a dozen articles representing the widest possible range of subjects and interests. Many of our contributors will be established historians whose books and essays are already well known to Canadian readers. Many others will be less familiar, but nonetheless stimulating, because one of our purposes is to encourage historical writing by articulate and perceptive non-professionals. Their articles will be suitably illustrated from the holdings of major Canadian and foreign archives in order to achieve an effect that is pleasing to the eye as well as to the mind.

Beginning with the serialization over the next three issues of George Grant's journey through the Rockies in 1883, we also intend to make the publication of period pieces and contemporary documents a permanent feature of the magazine. Finally, the magazine will carry reviews of recent Canadian books which, in our estimation, should be of interest to our readers. Our premises for selecting books for review will be entirely eclectic, going beyond history (*per se*) into art, architecture and other forms of cultural expression where the author's bias is, nevertheless, historical. We aspire, in short, to make *CANADA* a unique publication which will reflect the growing popularity, as any bookseller's shelves will testify, of Canadian history in the literary tastes and habits of Canadians.

The magazine has become a reality through cooperation between a major publishing house and a Canadian university in order to achieve a common goal: to foster wider interest in Canada's past, present and future. It is the sincere hope of everyone connected with *CANADA: An Historical Magazine* that our publication will make a contribution, however slight, to the achievement of that goal.

David Gagan
Editor

W.L. Mackenzie King and F.D.R. at Quebec City, 1936   *The Public Archives of Canada*

The Turning-Point: Canadian-American Relations during the Roosevelt-King Era
C.P.Stacey

The year 1933 brought to supreme power two politicians whose conjunction was to have a revolutionary effect on many matters, one of them being the relations of Canada and the United States. Adolf Hitler became Chancellor of Germany and Franklin Roosevelt was inaugurated as President of the United States.

The politician who was to lead Canada through the coming war was still in the wilderness. R. B. Bennett was Prime Minister and William Lyon Mackenzie King was leading the Opposition. The Roosevelt administration may have had a little to do with bringing King and the Liberals back to office. Its influence was exerted in a purely negative manner: it simply refrained from making a trade agreement with the Bennett government. Bennett, whose attitude on protective tariffs had changed considerably since his ministry's early days, wanted

an agreement, and had he got one his political position would have been improved, though it is hard to believe that he could possibly have won the election of 1935.

The day after that great Liberal victory at the polls, and before the new government had taken office, Norman Armour, the American Minister in Ottawa, had an interview with the Canadian Undersecretary of State for External Affairs, Dr. O. D. Skelton. Skelton was the most powerful civil servant in Canadian history, but he had not been quite so powerful during the last few years as he had been under the earlier King administration. He was undoubtedly delighted by the result of the election. At the same time he was deeply disturbed by the possibility of Canada being drawn into trouble as the result of the League of Nations' attempt to impose sanctions on Italy, which had lately attacked Ethiopia. Under these con-

1

ditions he perhaps let his hair down a little further than mandarins usually do. He seems to have told Armour that Canada was faced with a choice of alternatives: developing closer relations with the United States, or a closer union with the Empire. He made it clear that he himself, for both political and economic reasons, preferred the former. He remarked, incidentally, that he had not seen King recently.

King himself lost no time. He was sworn in as Prime Minister on 23 October 1935, and the next day he was beating on the American Minister's door. Armour, slightly embarrassed, had suggested that it was his place to call on the Prime Minister, but King came anyway, in spite of the fact that it was Thanksgiving Day. Armour's record of their conversation is interesting; it is clear that by now King had talked to Skelton:

> . . . Mr. King stressed the great importance of a successful trade agreement at this time on the relations between our two countries. He made it plain, as Dr. Skelton had done, that there were two roads open to Canada, but that he wanted to choose "the American road" if we made it possible for him to do so. From every point of view it was important that our attachments should be strengthened and our relations brought closer in every way, politically as well as economically. So strongly did he feel on this point that he even suggested that if I thought it would be welcomed or would help the situation he would be glad to consider proceeding himself to Washington and having a talk with the President.[1]

Armour and the State Department clearly felt that King was moving a bit fast. The Minister thought that his talk of visiting Washington was a gesture, not to be taken too seriously. Within a week, however, the plan for the visit was firm. The U.S. Legation cautiously hinted that there was no certainty that a trade agreement was within immediate reach, and that a misfire after a trip to Washington could be embarrassing. King was not deterred. On 8 November he was in the White House, and the following day — seventeen days after he had taken office — a trade agreement was privately initialled. It was signed, with much éclat, on 15 November.

The relationship between King and Roosevelt still needs investigation, and it is to be hoped that the biographical works on King now in preparation will throw some additional light upon it. But we must not expect too much. Neither Roosevelt nor King seems to me to have been exactly a monument of sincerity, and relations between two unusually insincere men present the historian with no ordinary problem. But whatever the motivation may have been on either side, it is hard to deny that under Roosevelt and King the Canadian-American relationship entered a new era, for better or for worse.

Franklin Roosevelt, the thirty-second President of the United States, was I think the first President of whom it could be said that he was genuinely popular in Canada. He was probably more popular with Canadians than Mackenzie King was, and certainly much more popular than R. B. Bennett. The reasons are, I think, fairly clear. The force of Roosevelt's personality defied national boundaries, just as Churchill's did. Canadians admired enormously the dynamism of his approach to the problems of the Depression. At the same time, however, he managed to make them feel that he was interested in and friendly to their country. This was so unusual that it enchanted them. Canadians, like some other North Americans, have an overwhelming desire to be loved; and when Roosevelt turned upon them the same powerful affability that served him so well at home, they felt that they were at last being loved as they deserved.

There was, of course, something else. From 1933 onwards it became increasingly evident that tigers were loose in the world. Very gradually, very reluctantly, Canadians began to realize that even remote Canada could be menaced; and the grim possibility presented itself that some day there would have to be an international tiger-hunt. One did not have to be a professional strategist to perceive the connection between the giant power next door and the security of Canada. It was possible also that Canada might have some importance in relation to the security of the United States; though the American professional strategists were more interested in other areas, notably Brazil.

Here we come across something definitely new. Except for small incidents in the First World War, which had left no permanent legacy, there had never been any military co-operation between Canada and the United States. Traditionally, of course, the two countries had been potential enemies, and there had been some quaint survivals of military preparation as late as the 1920's. When the Canadian Legation was opened in Washington no military attaché was appointed to it, and it may be said that there was no military contact of the slightest significance between the two governments until the Roosevelt-King era. The very earliest discussion of defence cooperation seems to have taken place between the President and the Prime Minister during King's visit to the White House in March 1937; and King's diary indicates that it was more slight and casual than he later liked to represent it as being. But in 1938 more happened. The United States Minister in Ottawa, the State Department and the President showed an interest in defence liaison with Canada. Everyone in Ottawa, I think it is fair to say, was in favour of it, but the Canadians cannily left the initiative to Washington. And as the result of a decision by Roosevelt, in January 1938 the Canadian Chiefs of Staff sneaked into the American capital. They came, under quite comic conditions of secrecy, to confer with their U.S. counterparts. That the meeting took place was more important than anything that happened during it. The Canadian officers' reports make it clear that the Americans, Admiral Leahy and General Craig, were quite puzzled about the whole thing. They clearly had felt no need for liaison with Canada and had not suggested it; they had no plans ready to discuss; and it even seems a little doubtful whether they knew that it was the President who had authorized the meeting. But the conversations were pleasant enough; some information was exchanged; and a precedent had been set.

Later in the year there were further developments. On 18 August Roosevelt made his first formal visit to Canada. The Czech crisis, which was to bring the world to the brink of war next month, was already grumbling on the horizon; and Roosevelt chose this moment to make the famous speech at Kingston in which he assured Canada that the United States would "not stand idly by" if the Dominion was threatened by an aggressor. Cordell Hull has recorded that the State Department wrote the speech, but that Roosevelt himself inserted that passage, the only part of it that had any importance. The new relationship was beginning to come out into the open.

Just over a year later war began. After going through the motions of neutrality for a week, Canada took her stand with the Allies, the only independent country in the Americas to do so. Mackenzie King had long known that such action was inevitable. With equal inevitability, the United States stood neutral. I need hardly recall, however, that this time its neutrality was very different from the sort that had jarred on Canadians in 1914-17. A small personal experience brought this home to me. As a reserve militia officer, I offered my services when war broke out. To my surprise, however, the Department of National Defence decided that it could conduct at least the first part of the war with Germany without my assistance; and so I went back to my teaching job at Princeton. In New York my wife and I had an hour to kill between trains; and we went to a newsreel theatre. The war was perhaps a fortnight old, and war scenes were beginning to come in from various places. Among them were some ineffably dull shots of the Canadian Militia grimly mobilizing. At these, to my utter amazement, the New York audience broke into warm applause. It was the only occasion in my memory when an American audience showed the slightest interest in Canada. A contemporary comment by the *New Yorker* said it all. I remember it as something like this: "The fact is, the American people hate Hitler and they want to see him soundly beaten by a couple of other fellows."

Nevertheless, the first consequence of war was to halt the promising rapprochement between Canada and the United States. During the first seven months of the war there was little or no contact between Roosevelt and King. But when the Allies began to suffer reverses it was actively resumed. King saw Roosevelt twice in April 1940, after the German invasion of Denmark and Norway. The Dunkirk evacuation and the collapse of France were staggering blows to complacency in North America: just how hard they hit the United States was reflected in the enactment of the draft law. It was these shocks to public confidence that finally brought Canada and the United States together. The statesmen had set the stage, but it was the threat of Nazi domination of Europe that produced decisive action.

If one must nominate a precise moment in time as the beginning of a new era, it is clearly the Ogdensburg meeting of 17-18 August 1940; and it is worthwhile to note just how this meeting came about. During that tremendous summer Canada and the United States had exchanged service attachés, a group of Canadian officers had visited Washington secretly to discuss cooperation, and Roosevelt had tried to use King to influence Churchill on no account to allow the British Fleet to pass into German hands — an incident that suggests just how pessimistic the President was about British chances at that moment. But at the beginning of August there was still no machinery for continuous high-level consultation on defence between the two countries, and in Canada, at least, a demand for such consultation was beginning to be heard.

American writers have suggested that Mackenzie King asked for the Ogdensburg meeting. It is clear, however, that he did not. His sure tactical sense did not desert him. He had been quite prepared to force the pace in the matter of a trade agreement, and he forced it later in

connection with the Hyde Park Declaration. On this much more important and ticklish question he waited for Roosevelt to move. And Roosevelt moved on 16 August. On that day the State Department sent him a letter from J. Pierrepont Moffat, who was now American Minister in Ottawa, reporting a public demand in Canada for "some form of defence understanding with the United States." Even elements once considered anti-American, Moffat said, "such as the Toronto public and the English-speaking sections of Montreal", were asking for this: "The old fear that cooperation with the United States would tend to weaken Canada's ties with Great Britain has almost entirely disappeared. Instead, Canada believes that such cooperation would tend to bring Britain and the United States closer together, rather than to force Britain and Canada apart."[2] It seems likely that it was this letter that led Roosevelt to act. At a press conference at noon that day he announced that in addition to holding conversations with Britain on the acquisition of new Western Hemisphere bases, his government was also having discussions with Canada on hemisphere defence. At the moment he said it, this was not precisely true; but very shortly afterwards he picked up the telephone and invited Mackenzie King to meet him at Ogdensburg the following day. King, needless to say, was delighted. On 18 August, exactly two years after Roosevelt's Kingston speech, the two men announced the establishment of a Permanent Joint Board on Defence to "consider in the broad sense the defence of the north half of the Western Hemisphere." This board has been functioning ever since.

A few points should be made about the Ogdensburg meeting. First: it was a purely political and civilian project. Although Colonel Stimson, his new Secretary of War, was with him at Ogdensburg, Roosevelt apparently had not consulted either the War or Navy Departments, and his military and naval advisers were as much taken by surprise as they had been by the conversations with the Canadian Chiefs of Staff in 1938. King on his side seems to have consulted nobody, military or civilian. The arrangement made at Ogdensburg was, essentially, between two men.

On the other hand, there has rarely been an international arrangement that was more universally applauded in the countries directly concerned. Its timing was a political masterpiece. The Canadian Department of External Affairs reported after surveying 37 Canadian newspapers and magazines, and 38 in the United Kingdom, that it had found simply no opposition to what was done at Ogdensburg. After some lapse of time, two or three Conservative politicians in Canada attempted to criticize the arrangement, mainly on the ground that it had the appearance of writing off Britain, whose forces were Canada's first line of defence. These attempts were damp squibs. In the United States the cheering was not quite so unanimous, but it was loud nevertheless. Having read 33 American newspapers, the Canadian officials wrote, "Some editors have criticized the form of the Agreement and certain isolationist papers have warned against its implications, but none have questioned its desirability from the point of view of hemisphere defence."[3]

How different the fortunes of the Ogdensburg arrangement were from those of the Albany project of 1910 when representatives of Canada and the United States met to forge the first reciprocity agreement in half a century. The chief reason, of course, is obvious. In 1910-11 there was in Canada a powerful imperial sentiment which on the whole was only strengthened by the increasingly threatening situation in Europe. This sentiment, certainly exploited to some extent by self-interested industrialists, combined with nationalism to defeat reciprocity. In 1940 there were probably few real imperialists left in Canada, even using the word in its mildest Canadian sense; but there were a great many people who believed in the British connection and the British Commonwealth, to say nothing of the cause for which the Commonwealth was fighting. In that grim moment, with the Commonwealth

looking into the pit of defeat, virtually all these people, as Moffat reported, favoured rapprochement with the United States. Such a relationship seemed the best hope of victory or even of survival.

One final point about Ogdensburg. Nobody signed a treaty there. Nobody signed anything. The Ogdensburg Declaration, as it came to be called, was a press release. It brought Canada and the United States into what amounted to a military alliance (which was, for sixteen months, an alliance between a belligerent and a neutral), but there was no firm definition of mutual responsibilities and commitments. There never has been, except so far as the North Atlantic Treaty of 1949, which the United States and Canada signed with ten other countries, has taken the place of a bilateral agreement. Few press releases have had such extensive consequences.

I do not propose to describe those consequences in detail. The alliance was and is, of course, a highly unequal affair. The exchanges of fulsome flattery that went on between Roosevelt and King tended to conceal this, but every so often the hard realities showed through. Witness for example the speed with which Roosevelt vetoed Churchill's tentative suggestion that King and the Canadian Chiefs of Staff should be given some active share in the Quebec Conference of 1943. The Canadian share was finally limited to providing the whiskey and soda. (This did not bother King as long as the Canadian voters were exposed to plenty of photographs of himself in company with Churchill and Roosevelt.) I commend to you also a letter which Mayor Fiorello LaGuardia, Chairman of the United States Section of the Permanent Joint Board on Defence, wrote to Roosevelt in May 1942. The subject was what came to be called the "Crimson" project, a colossal scheme for ferrying aircraft from the United States to Britain with the aid of airfields to be built in the Canadian north. The Little Flower wrote:

> . . . The plan . . . challenges imagination. It is so gigantic and dramatic. It took our

Canadian colleagues by surprise and frankly they have not yet recovered. We recessed until Monday and we must put it through on that day as every day now is precious.

We may encounter the usual difficulties because of pride and the little brother attitude with which you are familiar.

There is a remote chance that I may need your help Monday to get a phone call through to the Premier . . .[4]

The crisis that LaGuardia expected never happened, but his letter gives us a salutary glimpse of the facts of life.

In his conduct of relations with the United States, Mackenzie King remains as enigmatic as he is in any other area, which is saying a good deal. Many people would be tempted to say that when King privately declared his preference for "the American road" to Norman Armour in 1935, he revealed the governing principle of his life. And yet one must take into account the possibility that King was being no more sincere with the Americans than he was with other people, which again covers a good deal of ground. Perhaps, on the other hand, it is unfair to accuse King of insincerity. Perhaps he merely possessed an almost superhuman power of convincing himself of practically anything at practically any time. Mr. Pearson in his memoirs suggests that during the war Churchill and Roosevelt managed King by flattering his ego. From what I have myself read in the records, I should say this is profoundly true. I should say also that King, for whatever reasons — and I suspect they were largely atavistic — tended always to put a better construction on American actions towards Canada than he did on British actions; and that under the influence of Roosevelt's blarney he consistently failed to realize that Canada had in essence much greater influence in London than in Washington, and that he undervalued the support which the British government could almost always be prevailed on in a pinch to give to Canadian positions.

When one has said all this, one must also say that as the war proceeded King began to have considerable doubts as to whether the United

Mackenzie King, Churchill and F.D.R. at the Quebec Conference, 1943

6

States' intentions towards Canada were entirely honourable. Skelton, by this time, had gone to his reward, and it is impossible to say whether he would have encouraged these doubts or not. (Skelton, after all, was capable of learning by experience; in the summer of 1940 he suddenly discovered that the best place to defend Canada was the beaches of England rather than the suburbs of Halifax.) Be this as it may, we find King on various occasions recording his anxiety over American activities in Canada, particularly in the north, and over the possibility of "efforts that would be made by the Americans to control developments in our country after the war, and to bring Canada out of the orbit of the British Commonwealth of Nations into their own orbit". In 1943 Malcolm MacDonald, the British High Commissioner, who enjoyed an unusual degree of King's confidence, had little difficulty, after a visit to the Northwest, in convincing King and the Cabinet War Committee that a potentially menacing situation existed there. It was now that a Special Commissioner was appointed with instructions to watch over and safeguard Canadian sovereignty in that region.

During the postwar years of his administration, 1945-48, King's anxieties persisted. In 1946, disturbed by happenings in the Permanent Joint Board on Defence, he told the Cabinet he "believed the long range policy of the Americans was to absorb Canada." After speaking of U.S. activity in the north, he went on, "It might be inevitable for us to have to submit to it — being so few in numbers and no longer able to look to British power for protection." That *cri de coeur* is revealing both about King and about the Canadian situation. The joint statement issued in February 1947 about the continuance of the Permanent Joint Board, with its emphasis on "limited" collaboration and preservation of national sovereignty, is a typical King document. In King's last months in office in 1948 much attention centred on a highly confidential proposal from Washington for reciprocal free trade. At first King favoured it; but almost immediately he developed doubts.

He ended up by talking like Sir John A. Macdonald in 1891: "I told Pearson that while I might miss to be the head of the Government, I would never cease to be a Liberal or a British citizen and if I thought there was a danger of Canada being placed at the mercy of powerful financial interests in the United States, and if that was being done by my own party, I would get out and oppose them openly."[5]

There is a great deal more one might say of Mackenzie King, but here perhaps we should take leave of him. He resigned in November 1948, and thereafter Louis St. Laurent, and Mike Pearson, and the boys in External Affairs, who King thought had "become imbued with the attention they have received from the Americans", had things their own way. It would be true to say that they took the country further down the American road than King had ever done, but it can be said with equal force that they ended the era of isolation and accepted the idea that in a dangerous world Canada should be prepared to accept her due share of national responsibility for collective defence. Under the influence of the Cold War and the dreadful menace of the hydrogen bomb, military commitments to the United States proliferated, both within and outside the sphere of the North Atlantic Treaty Organization. In 1957 a new Conservative government agreed to the joint creation of the North American Air Defence Command. All these things may be said to go back to Ogdensburg, which inaugurated the era of military collaboration.

To use a good old-fashioned pomposity, perhaps it is still too early to assess Ogdensburg. In 1940 almost everybody cheered. Today Americans, after their fashion, have forgotten it. On this side, a fair number of Canadians, particularly young ones, would probably say now that Ogdensburg was merely a stage in the great national sell-out. I find myself remembering almost the only statesmen of eminence on our side of the war who took a poor view of it at the time. Mackenzie King was inexpressibly shocked when Winston Churchill made it evident that he had no enthusiasm at all for what

"Mackenzie" and Franklin had been up to. No doubt Winston, as a good late-Victorian, was merely distressed to see one of the King's great colonies apparently slipping away, one of the jewels in the crown loosening in its socket. We more sophisticated people can look at the event in terms of what it meant for Canada as a nation. As a supposedly sophisticated student of history, I should probably conceal a private suspicion I entertain. I suspect that that character we used to call the future historian may ultimately conclude that the worst blow Canadian nationality ever suffered was the decline of the British Empire, which Winston was so determined not to preside over. Indeed, Mackenzie King seems to have been moving towards this view in his last years. After all, let us remember, he was a late Victorian too; though so far as I know he never rode in a cavalry charge, and it seems unlikely that anyone will ever make a movie about him called Young Billy.

When the "future historian" looks at the Canadian-American events of 1940, his judgment will doubtless be swayed by the course of things between our time and his. I am sorry to end on a sombre note. We are perhaps too much disposed to simplify our problems. We sometimes talk as if Canada and the United States were alone in the world. We are not alone; and the world today is not the world in which they held the great election in Missinaba County in 1911. Nor, indeed, is it the world in which King and Roosevelt met on the St. Lawrence in 1940. Mankind has been living on borrowed time ever since the bomb went down on Hiroshima in 1945, and in spite of the current thaw in the Cold War we still live under the shadow of nameless and horrible menaces. Today nobody has more than limited freedom of choice in foreign policy. This does not mean that Canada will necessarily be absorbed by the United States, as Mackenzie King feared, or that we shall not still contrive to exist as separate mutually-respecting national entities. But Canada and the United States are both potentially at the mercy of situations which neither can control and which Canada can do little even to influence. In 1940 world events dropped us in the same boat, willy-nilly. In a future world crisis, I do not think it is possible to doubt that we should inevitably be in the same boat again. Perhaps it would be more accurate to say, we shall be in the same boat — if there is a boat.

Footnotes

This paper was originally prepared for, and read to, the 7th Northern Great Plains History Conference at Winnipeg, October 1972.

1. *Foreign Relations of the United States: Diplomatic Papers, 1935*, II (Washington, 1952), 27-30.

2. *Ibid., 1940*, III (Washington, 1958), 144-5.

3. C. P. Stacey, *Arms, Men and Governments: The War Policies of Canada, 1939-1945* (Ottawa, 1970), 340 (from King Papers).

4. *Ibid.*, 375 (from Roosevelt Papers).

5. J. W. Pickersgill and D. F. Forster, *The Mackenzie King Record*, IV (Toronto, 1970), 273.

Note On Sources

The trade negotiations of 1935 (including Armour's interview with Skelton) are described in Richard N. Kottman, *Reciprocity and the North Atlantic Triangle, 1932-1938* (Ithaca, N.Y., 1968). For the development of the military relationship between Canada and the United States, including the background of the Ogdensburg meeting and Churchill's reaction to it, see C.P. Stacey, *Arms, Men and Governments: The War Policies of Canada, 1939-1945* (Ottawa, 1970), which is fully documented. The American side of the story is in Stanley W. Dziuban, *Military Relations between the United States and Canada, 1939-1945* (Washington, 1959). A great deal about King can be learned from J.W. Pickersgill and D.F. Forster, *The Mackenzie King Record* (4 vols., Toronto, 1960-70).

How New France Might Have Become New Holland

Jan Kupp

In 1603, Pierre du Gua, Sieur de Monts, formed a trading company for the purpose of establishing "an orderly and gainful" trade in Canada protected by a monopoly which the French government had granted in order to encourage the colonization of its colony in North America. Since 1584, several attempts had been made to organize a company which would have sufficient financial backing and experienced personnel to make the fur trade in Canada a success and at the same time establish a settlement in the colony. All these efforts had ended in disaster either because some interested parties in France had been excluded or because the leaders of the enterprise had little or no experience. A monopoly trade in newly discovered regions was a necessity. It excluded murderous competition for a company which had to bear the heavy expenses of exploration and of transporting settlers and maintaining them for the first years until they became independent of the company's support. None of the European governments interested in the acquisition of colonies was willing or able to subsidize the costs of settling their newly acquired territories and therefore granted trade monopolies in the regions concerned.

The company of de Monts was the first French undertaking potentially capable of developing the Canadian fur trade, and at the same time capable of providing and sustaining settlers, because it had a strong financial basis and the backing of all the French Atlantic ports interested in this trade: Rouen, Honfleur, St. Malo and La Rochelle. It took the precaution of sending a geographer, Samuel Champlain, and an experienced fur trader, François du Pont Gravé, to Canada in order to find the most suitable site for the Company's trade. When the choice fell on the Bay of Fundy the Company sailed with its fleet of four ships to

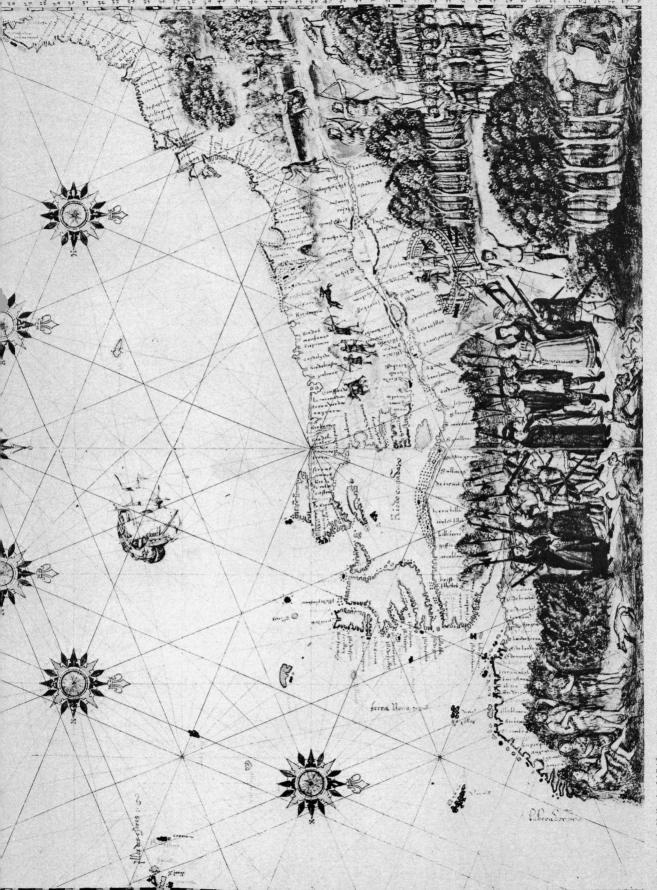

Canada in 1604, and settled first at the St. Croix River and shortly afterwards at Port Royal. The trade with the Indians was rewarding. The settlers found suitable soil for growing food and wintered with success. Everything pointed to a good start for the development of Canada when, suddenly, disaster struck. In the summer of 1606, a heavily armed Dutch ship seized half of the Company's fleet, commandeered the cargoes of their furs and equipment and left the French company bankrupt. This was not an isolated accident which could happen to any commercial enterprise in distant waters. The raid on the Monts' company was part of a determined policy of a well-organized group of Amsterdam merchants who intended to make themselves master of the Canadian fur trade.

The Dutch traders had very good reasons for their attack on the French fur trade in Canada. The religious wars of the last quarter of the sixteenth century had driven many of the more important fur traders of Central and Western Europe to the Netherlands where they found a refuge first in Antwerp and, after its sack by the Spanish armies in 1585, in the city of Amsterdam. They had made a successful effort to displace the English merchants from the good graces of the Russian tsar and soon gained a dominant position in Archangel, the main export harbour for Russian beaver and other furs. This favourable position, acquired at great cost, was almost immediately threatened by the Canadian furs which a well-organized French company could provide for the European market. It was, therefore, of the utmost importance to ruin such a company before it had reached a strong financial position or, if this should prove to be impossible, to gain control of its operations. Both of these policies had proved successful in the past. By these means the Dutch previously had discouraged competition, for example, from the herring fisheries in the English Channel and the spice trade in the Celebes Islands. The Dutch raid on the Monts' Company, conducted at a time when France and Holland were close allies, was

Champlain according to a contemporary engraving
The Public Archives of Canada

the first salvo in the war for the Canadian furs. A group of Amsterdam merchants and capitalists first determined to ruin the fur trade of the French company by equipping a heavily armed man-of-war to plunder the French ships and the Tadoussac trade. This strategy succeeded and de Monts and his partners were driven into bankruptcy. Only a direct protest from the French King, Henry IV, to the Dutch States General prevented a complete take-over of the North American beaver trade, important for the fast-developing beaver hat industry of France. The Amsterdam merchants were not easily discouraged, however, even though they had to abandon their policy of armed harassment. After 1607, they adopted the more subtle and thoroughly modern strategy of corporate take-over.

Sufficient information with regard to the operations of the Canadian fur trade, capital investment and other data had been amassed by the Dutch from sympathetic participants of the Monts Company, the Dutchman Cornelis de Bellois and Guillaume Chevalier. Bellois was one of a large number of Dutch merchants who, since the end of the sixteenth century, had settled in Rouen. Many of them were engaged in the beaver hat industry. Bellois had frenchified his Dutch name and married a niece of Boyer, another partner of the Company of de Monts. In 1603, or early in 1604, the Dutchman had joined Boyer in the Canadian fur trade enterprise. Chevalier kept close business relations with Bellois. Early in 1606, Champlain received warnings that Chevalier might be in the pay of foreign interests and he therefore kept a close watch on the latter's activities when the trader visited Port Royal. Bellois and Chevalier certainly were both trading for their own account in Canada at the expense of their company, and most probably on behalf of the Dutch fur traders. De Monts apparently was suspicious because immediately after the Dutch raid he revoked the special trading powers he had given Bellois several years before. In short, from the numerous French notarial contracts of the years 1604-1607 it appears that the ability of the Dutch to penetrate the Canadian trade was greatly facilitated by dissatisfied elements among the Company's fur traders who, for reasons of their own, thought that they were not receiving their proper share of the trade.

One of the more conspicuous merchants who decided to cooperate with the Dutch was the close associate of Champlain and lieutenant of de Monts, François du Pont Gravé. Pont Gravé was born in November, 1560 in St. Malo. He was a member of the numerous and influential Gravé family which had lived in St. Malo for more than a century. His father and uncles had many commercial ties with Middelburg and Veere, two harbour towns in Zeeland, the southwestern part of Holland. When Champlain, in 1603, made his first journey to Canada he was accompanied by Pont Gravé. According to the explorer, the French trader was well-known among the Indians and had traded in Tadoussac many years before the formation of the Monts Company. In his later journeys Champlain mentioned him with some affection and worried about the trader's health when the latter was affected by severe attacks of rheumatism. This close association lasted until the

early 1620's when Pont Gravé withdrew from active trading in Canada because of ill-health. His position in Canada was that of main trader of the Company as well as interpreter and adviser to Champlain. At first he seemed to have been devoted to the Monts Company, but by 1608 Dutch infiltration, combined with the disastrous financial results of the raid on the Company in 1606, produced a serious decline in Pont Gravé's private fortunes. Moreover, what little harmony had existed among the traders participating in the Canadian company before 1606 had completely disappeared.

By 1606, trading outside the Company and double-crossing each other had become the order of the day. Bellois, assisted by Chevalier, seized the goods and merchandise of Pont Gravé on November 16, 1606, a few months after the raid of the Dutch merchants on de Monts' ships in Tadoussac. In September, 1607, the Great Council of France condemned Bellois and his associates ordering them to return the goods seized from Pont Gravé and to pay the latter 1500 *livres* for the loss of interest and damages. Appeal procedures delayed the payment of these reparations, however, and in the meantime, as if to make a bad situation worse, the Rochelle firm of Georges and Macain, who were the financial backers of de Monts (but also the associates of the Dutch Northern Company operating in the whale fisheries of the Arctic), seized Pont Gravé's furs brought from Canada during the year 1607. Then, in October 1607, Pont Gravé himself was accused by de Monts of trading illegally in Tadoussac. De Monts ordered Pont Gravé's store of furs, 1224 beaver skins, to be seized in retaliation. From all appearances there was little honour among thieves and under these circumstances the associate and friend of Champlain had to acquire credit in order to continue his trading in Canada. Ready reserves of cash were especially important in 1608, when it became certain that De Monts' monopoly would be revoked thereby opening the fur trade of Canada to all interested parties. The revocation of De Monts' monopoly was the direct result of a change in French economic policies in 1608.

From the memoirs of Henry IV and his first minister, Sully, it appears that since the beginning of the century the French King had been laying careful plans for making France once more a leading European nation. The execution of his policies demanded a strong economy and a sizable merchant navy. Because Holland, his ally against the powerful German and Spanish House of Hapsburg, was well on its way to becoming the commercial empire of the seventeenth century, Henry approached several prominent Dutch merchants, for example, Isaac le Maire and Balthasar de Moucheron. Their task would be the reorganization of the French economy and the building of a strong merchant fleet. These activities brought the King into direct conflict with the Dutch Republic which was constantly on guard against possible French and English competition. The Dutch States General in 1607, in their reply to the French protest against the raid on the Canadian Company, had told the King that they would stop a repetition of this attack by their subjects but would not recognize any restrictions on their freedom of trade. When Henry IV, through his ambassador in Holland, continued his efforts to recruit Dutch personnel for building a merchant fleet, the States General issued a decree warning that all Dutchmen who entered the service of France would be hanged from the highest yardarm. This refusal of Dutch cooperation, and other factors, completely changed the King's plans. In one of his letters to the Dutch ambassador in France Henry, anxious to maintain good relations with Holland, explained that it had never been his intention to forbid Dutch merchants to participate in French enterprises nor to hinder Dutch commerce in any other form. The result of this statement was the end of the trading monopoly in Canada and an acceleration of Dutch participation in the Canadian fur trade. From that moment, Dutch interest in the person of Pont Gravé noticeably increased.

In 1608, it was not difficult for Pont Gravé, still closely connected with the French Company, to find in Rouen persons who were willing to help him out of his financial difficulties. Considering his experience and knowledge of the fur trade of Canada the trader would be a valuable asset to foreign commercial interests. Rouen was and remained for many years the principal market for the Canadian beaver. In this Norman town lived a numerous and prosperous colony of Dutch merchants who had settled there during the 1590's. There are no indications whom Pont Gravé approached but, considering his actions, it seems likely that it may have been Jacob Eelkens, a prominent fur trader of Rouen and an agent of the great Amsterdam fur trading house of Arnout Vogels. The latter was a shareholder of the international fur company of Jabach established in Cologne. What is certain is that on January 4, 1608 Pont Gravé asked for and received a loan from the Paris branch of the Jabach Company. On that date he signed a declaration before some Paris notaries that he had received the sum of 1190 *livres* and 5 sous from Mathys Duysterloo and Jan Honthom, the agents of Jabach in the French capital. The loan was intended to equip two ships destined for the trade with the Indians of Tadoussac and Campseau. It was a bottomry loan or, as the French called it an "*emprunt a la grosse aventure de la mer.*" This meant that the money was loaned on ship and merchandise to be paid back only when the ships returned safely. Therefore there was a considerable risk involved and, considering the destination of the two ships, the interest of twenty-five percent was not high. Journeys to little-frequented waters usually demanded a higher interest rate often running as high as thirty-five percent. As far as we can ascertain the Jabach firm was not in the bottomry loan business. Its willingness to provide the loan on reasonable terms may have been influenced by a desire to acquire the co-operation of Pont Gravé. Be that as it may, the fur trader became a regular customer of Jabach. On February 25, 1609 Pont Gravé again borrowed for the same purpose and in the same manner the sum of 1000 *livres*. Apparently the trading had been a success and the French fur trader's credit was established. On December 23, 1609 he received another loan from Jabach. This time the Frenchman borrowed 772 *livres* but instead of having to pay twenty-five percent interest he was now asked to bring back one hundred good, new beaver skins and deliver them to Duysterloo as full payment for loan and interest within a fortnight after his return from Canada. There is no direct proof, but it seems reasonable to assume that Duysterloo had demanded Pont Gravé's cooperation in return for these loans. The involvement of the French trader with the Jabach agency is all the more remarkable because, in 1608, he was still an associate of de Monts who conducted the Canadian trade under a one year monopoly until 1609 in order to make good his losses suffered because of the Dutch raid. It was also the year when Champlain was engaged in the building of his habitation at Quebec — the first step in the creation of a "new" France. To form an idea of the complications inherent in this involvement of Pont Gravé with Jabach, we must consider for a moment connections of the Dutch moneylenders.

The Jabach Company was an old and well-established trading concern of Cologne with large interests in Central and Eastern European commerce. Its various merchandise included furs which it received from Russia, Poland and the northern Baltic regions via Leipzig, Frankfurt and other fur markets. It may have been a coincidence, but the expansion of the firm's interests into the capitals of Western Europe began at a time when North American furs first appeared sporadically on the Rouen market. In the 1570's Jaback opened an agency in Antwerp. This was followed, in 1600, by the establishment of a Paris branch. The date of the opening of a branch in Amsterdam is not known but probably coincided with the arrival of one of the Company's major shareholders, Hendrick Duysterloo, in the Dutch city during the early 1590's.

To comprehend the widespread tentacles of the Jabach firm, one has to study the genealogical register of the family. The great mer-

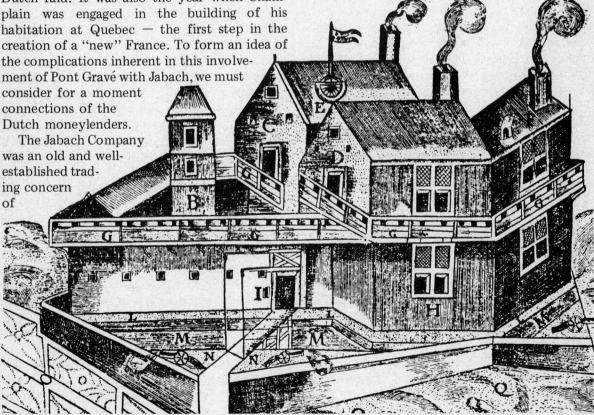

The Habitation in Quebec, 1608-1624   *The Public Archives of Canada*

chant houses followed the same practice as the royal dynasties. By marriage they expanded their influence and formed commercial alliances in many countries. Their relatives served as agents who provided commercial information, facilitated financial transactions, spied on rivals and were especially useful at times when trade was blocked or seriously hindered by governments of countries hostile to that of the mother firm. By marriage the Jabachs were connected with the Honthoms, the Duysterloos, the Vogels, the Pelts and other important Dutch merchant families with enterprises all over the European continent. The Vogels worked closely together with the Eelckens of Rouen and Amsterdam. They traded exclusively in furs which may have been the reason for the early interest of Vogels in the New York fur trade. The Duysterloos traded in Amsterdam, Germany and the Baltic mainly in furs and leather. The Honthoms at first concentrated on the fur trade but later expanded their interest to include other commodities. However, one still meets their name in many fur contracts of the late seventeenth century. The Pelts, the in-laws of Vogels, dealt mainly in furs and fish but their trade was oriented primarily towards Norway and Russia. Branches of these families were to be found from Constantinople to Archangel. They were the Renaissance equivalent, in effect, of the modern multinational corporation. The religious wars of the late sixteenth century brought these families from Germany to Antwerp and later to Holland where they settled principally in Amsterdam.

The head office of Jabach was in Cologne, a free city of the Holy Roman Empire. In 1600, the firm considered that it needed more working capital. A new subscription brought in more capital to the amount of 330,000 guilders or almost three quarter of a million *livres*. This was equal to one sixth of the total capital of either of the two great trading companies of that time, the English and Dutch East India Companies, and the equivalent of almost forty million dollars of our present money. Clearly the Jabach Company was a large-scale operation. It may be coincidental, but this new capitalization occurred just when the first serious attempts were made towards the development of the Canadian fur trade. The goal of any commercial enterprise, then as now, is to acquire a monopoly of the trade of those commodities in which the particular firm specializes. Modern governments employ legislation to prevent the formation of cartels and trusts. But the merchants of the seventeenth century were a law unto themselves and did not hesitate, as the raid of 1606 clearly demonstrates, to use violence against possible competitors. As has already been mentioned, Canadian furs of exceptional quality appeared at this time in considerable numbers on the Rouen market. Understandably, Jabach and associates, whose old Russian-based monopoly in the European fur trade was seriously threatened by this new source of fur supplies, were worried. One could expect them to increase their efforts to make themselves master of the Canadian furs. The period of free trade in Canada after 1610 provided them with a golden opportunity.

Thus, on June 24, 1611 three merchants formed a company in Amsterdam in order to trade in Canada. Its headquarters were established in Rouen to avoid the difficulties which faced foreigners trading in a French colony. The contract was drawn up in Amsterdam before a Dutch notary. The first partner, a resident of this Dutch city, was the younger Arnout Vogels who had served his apprenticeship in the fur trade in the firm of Hendrick Duysterloo and had strong trade relations with Rouen. The second party was Jehan Andries or Jean Andrieu, a merchant of Honfleur, at that time a prosperous harbour at the mouth of the Seine, not far from Rouen, and the point of departure for most ships sailing to Canada. The third party was Lodewyck Vermeulen (or Vermille as he is called in French documents), a member of the Dutch colony of Rouen. Vermeulen and Andrieu were in charge of the operations in Rouen and Canada. Vogels took charge of the buying of merchandise for the trade and did so presumably in Amsterdam because the prices of French goods was at that time already higher than those of Holland. Most surprising is that the new company's agent in charge of the Canadian trade, indeed a profit-sharing partner, was none other than François du Pont Gravé, now heavily indebted to Duysterloo, Vogels and Honthom, all connected with the great Jabach firm and family.

Because the contract stipulated that if Pont Gravé could not make the voyage to America his partners in Rouen were entitled to engage a substitute who would earn a share of Pont Gravé's profits, it would seem that the Frenchman's Canadian experience and contacts were of signal importance to the company. Indeed, he was asked to contribute nothing else. The other partners each undertook to contribute one third of the costs of ship and merchandise. The trading in Canada must have been profitable because two years later, in another contract, we meet the same partners again. On this occasion Arnout Vogels, in order to meet certain financial difficulties, sold his one-third share to his brothers-in-law Abraham and Hans Pelt of Amsterdam. The Company's ship for which Vogels had provided the cargo had sailed some weeks before — late March or early April — from Honfleur to Canada under the command of Pont Gravé. That Vogels could deed his rights to the Pelts indicates that the trade was continuing at a good profit. The Pelts were known as shrewd merchants and would not have taken over Vogels share in the Canadian trade if it had not promised a good return for their money. The Pelts were closely connected with the Russian fur trade and the developing fur trade of the Hudson and Delaware Rivers. Therefore they could be expected to be familiar with all the aspects of the trade. In the 1613 contract, Pont Gravé is again mentioned as an important asset in the Company's activities in Canada. It is perhaps worthwhile to follow his movements in the years 1611 and 1613.

In the *Works of Champlain* it is mentioned that the explorer returned from Canada to France in the fall of 1610. Pont Gravé returned with him because "trade was poor" as a result of the presence of numerous free traders in the St. Lawrence. De Monts, meanwhile, had bought out his former partners who refused to be financially involved in the Canadian trade without a monopoly. Nevertheless, Champlain and Pont Gravé apparently stayed with de Monts since they remained closely together during the trading in Canada in the free trade period which lasted until the fall of 1612. In the spring of 1611 Pont Gravé and Champlain returned to the St. Lawrence where Pont Gravé acted out his role as a double agent for the first time. Champlain, who seems to have been completely unaware of Pont Gravé's duplicity, reported that the trade was poor in 1610 and in the following two years as well; but during the same period, as we have mentioned, the Dutch company apparently received good returns. Pont Gravé was probably in actual command of French trading operations at this time, for Champlain states clearly that he returned to France in September of 1611, with the approval of the old fur trader. Before Champlain's departure, however, he joined Pont Gravé at the Lachine Rapids near Montreal. The trading at Tadoussac had been poor and Pont Gravé, followed by a large number of free traders, bartered during the following weeks with many Indians who had gathered at the Rapids. Trade was recorded as very light. On July 11, 1611, Pont Gravé left Champlain in order to attend to some business at Tadoussac. According to the Dutch contract, it was at this time that the ship of Pont Gravé's Dutch partners was expected to arrive in the St. Lawrence. The inevitable conclusion is that Pont Gravé travelled to Tadoussac to meet the Dutch ship with a consignment of the best furs while Champlain remained with the Indians at the Rapids. But what could have been the reason for Pont Gravé's betrayal of de Monts and Champlain?

For one thing, the veteran fur trader had little reason to put his trust in the fortunes of de Monts, a bankrupt, and Champlain, a dreamer. Champlain may have been an attractive person as an individual but his dreams of exploration, settlement, and the conversion of the Indians had little meaning for an old experienced trader who equated New France only with the possibilities and risks of the fur trade. The old de Monts' Company was deeply involved in lawsuits before several French courts. It had not even received the 6000 *livres* which the French treasury had been ordered in 1608 to pay as compensation for the loss of the Company's monopoly. In short, de Monts' organization, deeply in debt, could no longer command the loyalty of the impecunious fur trader, especially after it lost its special trading rights.

Pont Gravé's illicit activities became even more pronounced in 1613 when free trade came to an end and Canada once more became the property of a monopoly company. In 1612, Champlain had been appointed lieutenant of the Prince de Condé, recently named Viceroy of Canada. In February 1613, the explorer made an agreement with the old partners of de Monts for the establishment of a new monopoly company for the fur trade in Canada, an organization often called the Champlain Company. Among the contractors were Boyer who also signed for Pont Gravé, Bellois and Pont Gravé's Dutch trading partner, Louis Vermeulen. All had played a part in the earlier Dutch infiltration of the Canadian trade. When Louis Vermeulen became a director of the Champlain Company in 1613, the influence of the Dutch fur trade now reached into the policy-making body of the French Company. De Monts remained in the background as a shareholder and no longer took any active part in the Canadian fur trade. For his part, Champlain seems to have been oblivious to both the extent and the implications of Dutch participation in his company.

Champlain left Honfleur for Canada on March 5, 1613. He sailed in the ship of Pont Gravé. If we may believe his account of some twenty years later, Pont Gravé actually kept him company during the journey to the colony. It is clear from his writing that Champlain had no suspicion that Pont Gravé in fact sailed as an agent for the Dutch Company on a ship bought by the Company with a cargo provided by Arnout Vogels. To make matters even more complicated, the double-dealing had been duly legalized before a French notary. On February 5, 1613 an agreement was made between Champlain, acting for the Viceroy of Canada, and two other parties, Mathieu Georges, representing the merchants of La Rochelle, and Daniel Boyer, representing those of Rouen, for the organization of the Champlain Company. It was stipulated that de Monts and Vermeulen would equip a ship of one hundred tons for the voyage to Canada. From the description of the ship in the Dutch contract and her tonnage it seems that she was the property of the Vermeulen-Vogels-Andrieu-Pont Gravé Company. Unwittingly, Champlain had given a trading licence to the Dutch Company in the belief that he was dealing with the old de Monts organization. It is certain from the Dutch document that the ship left Honfleur in the early spring of 1613, traded in Canada and made good profits.

The 1613 situation indicated that the Dutch merchants had acquired a considerable foothold in the Canadian beaver trade. It is impossible to state how far they were financially involved because the amount of their participation is unknown. It must have been substantial, otherwise they could not have exercised the degree of control that they did. Neither Pont Gravé nor the other partners of the Champlain Company were men of means, and it is a fact that a short while later Mathys Duysterloo, the Paris agent of Jabach, joined Vermeulen as a director of the Champlain Company. This fact strengthens the suspicion that Pont Gravé, perhaps even de Monts himself, and certainly Vermeulen were merely fronting for the Dutch interests centred in Amsterdam and Cologne. Their "business first" attitude soon became evident. For example, when Champlain tried to force the Company's directors to increase the funds allotted for settlement and the conversion of the natives, Vermeulen and Duysterloo simply vetoed all extra expenditures not immediately related to the trade.

When Champlain persisted, insisting at the same time that the settlers be allowed to trade freely in furs and that the Company should function only as a counting house, the directors replied in 1620 by excluding Champlain from all matters concerning the fur trade. He was even forbidden to enter the Company's warehouse. Still, Champlain remained quite oblivious to the influence of the Dutch behind these machinations. Ironically, he was preoccupied with the visible Dutch danger on his flank at Fort Orange, now Albany. In 1615 this trading station received 2500 furs from the Hudson River area alone. When Champlain staged an attack on the Iroquois who acted as middlemen for the Dutch in the interior of the continent, he met with stony indifference, and received no cooperation, from his Company's traders. They seem to have considered him useful only as a figurehead, particularly when it came to seeking favours and protection at the French court. Through all this, Pont Gravé remained dutifully at Champlain's side.

There is no indication when the Dutch Company which had been created in 1611 to infiltrate the Canadian fur trade ceased to operate. Most probably the partnership was dissolved by 1615. By then, the partners were deeply involved in other ventures. Jean Andrieu had become associated with a company operating in Brazil. Vogels and the Pelts were involved in the New Netherland Company which had acquired a monopoly over the region drained by the Hudson and Delaware Rivers. In any case, with Vermeulen and Duysterloo firmly established in the directorate of the Champlain Company there was no longer any need for shadow companies in Holland.

If the Father of New France allowed himself to be a pawn of the Dutch, refusing to recognize the dangers inherent in their participation in the Canadian monopoly, other observers were fully aware of the implications. The French economist Antoine de Montchrétien, in his *Traicte de l'Oeconomie Politique* published in 1615, described the highly aggressive economic policies of the Dutch Republic and the growing subjection of the French economy to Dutch mercantile interests; and he warned of the serious danger that the Dutch would soon be in a position to take over the fur trade of Canada, if not the colony itself. According to Champlain's memoirs of 1632, the French intendant Dollu, responsible to the Ministry of Trade and Commerce, reported in 1620 that the directors of the Champlain Company intended to hand over control of the Company and the colony to certain foreigners. Considering the composition of the directorate this could only refer to the Dutch fur interests, in particular the Jabach firm. Years later when the Company of New France was formed from members of the Company of One Hundred Associates, Mathys Duysterloo was openly accused of exercising complete control of the Canadian beaver trade, having acquired the majority of the shares of the latter company. Yet, except for the above-mentioned remark, Champlain remained silent on all these events. His continuing friendship with Pont Gravé seems to indicate that he was unaware of being double-crossed; nor did he ever voice any suspicion about the presence of Vermeulen and Duysterloo in the directorate of the Company. One may conclude that the Father of New France was indeed an idealist with little business sense.

Montchrétien was merely the first of a long line of economists and politicians who would echo his warnings about foreign take-over of the Canadian economy. He, however, had one consolation. His warning was heeded. In 1621, the Dutch directors and their sympathizers were removed from the Canadian Company and a new directorate was appointed consisting solely of Frenchmen who had no immediate connections with the Dutch trade. The merchants of the old Company were allowed to remain as shareholders but without any participation in the actual trade. Whether they accepted this condition is doubtful because their successors in the Canadian trade were continuously short of financial resources. In 1627, Cardinal Richelieu took one more step towards complete nationalization of the Canadian fur trade. Henceforward, only Frenchmen and Roman Catholics were permitted to participate; but it was only through intimidation and great political pressure that the strong man of France secured the necessary domestic capital. Since the discovery of Canada there had never been much eagerness among the French merchants to share in the development of the colony. Richelieu discovered that this attitude had not changed. Future events justified their caution. From 1627 to 1763 Canada's development — what little there was of it — became a financial morass which in 1759 alone cost the French government sixty million *livres*.

In the meantime, true to their principle of never gambling on one source of supplies, the Dutch merchants had found and exploited a profitable alternative to the Canadian fur trade. From New York they conducted a murderous competition for the Canadian beaver and other furs until 1664. At the same time they kept control of the Russian fur market. Dutch competition thus served as an effective check on the price of French exports with potentially ruinous results, as the Canadian fur glut of 1690-1720 would demonstrate.

Might New France have become New Holland if the Dutch merchants had succeeded in their plans? In view of present-day parallels this is a question to challenge the Canadian imagination.

Notes on Sources

The primary sources consulted in the preparation of this article include Volumes IX and X of the Collection of Dutch Documents, relating to the early cod fisheries and fur trade in North America, in the Public Archives of Canada; the Notarial Archives which are part of the Municipal Archives of Amsterdam. Printed primary sources include H. P. Biggar, ed., *Works of Samuel de Champlain* (Toronto, 1925) and R. LeBlant and R. Baudry, eds., *Nouveaux Documents sur Champlain et son Epoque* (Ottawa, 1967). Secondary sources of related interest include: Peter Paul Trippen, *Jabach, die "Fugger" Familie des Westen* (Cologne, 1936); Simon Hart, *The Prehistory of the New Netherland Company* (Amsterdam, 1959); and Jan Kupp, "La Dissolution de la Compagnie du M. de Monts, 1607," *Revue d'histoire de l'Amerique française* (December, 1970). The most recent biography of Champlain is Samuel Eliot Morison, *Samuel de Champlain, Father of New France* (Boston, Toronto, 1972).

Robert Gourlay: Upper Canada's Banished Traitor

Lois Darroch Milani

hat, in your opinion, retards the development of your township, and what would most contribute to the same?" That question sounds innocent enough today, but in 1817 when Robert Gourlay asked Upper Canadian township officials to answer it, it was construed to be seditious libel. For asking the question Gourlay was imprisoned and, finally, banished from the province on pain of death if he returned.

Who was Robert Gourlay, and who were the people who gave so sinister an implication to such an innocuous question? Under what circumstances did he flash across the province like a meteor in 1818, twice tried and acquitted for seditious libel while the rafters of the courthouse rang with shouts of "Gourlay Forever?" What had shaped the character and attitudes of this forty-year-old man who felt compelled to challenge the authority of the provincial government in a one-man crusade against oligarchy. What had prompted him, in another setting, to so offend the Earl of Kellie that he

left his native Scotland in 1810? What made him persist in antagonizing his landlord, the Duke of Somerset, and the other great landowners of Wiltshire? And why, when he returned to Britain after his banishment from Canada, was he imprisoned on a charge of insanity? Was he really insane, or was it merely expedient to treat political eccentrics as madmen?

Canadian history books have treated Robert Gourlay, when they acknowledge him at all, as a misguided malcontent perhaps deservedly drummed out of the province as an irresponsible troublemaker. We see him now as a force in himself, a single-minded crusader in the cause of the common man at a time when ordinary men in Britain and in British North America were beginning to challenge the power and the ideology of the ruling elite. Gourlay came to Upper Canada, after a stormy career in Britain, to find reform in the air but no organized forces of reform; and he became the catalyst of a brief political revolt that fanned the flames of reform and set the stage for those developments which, over the next two decades, permanently altered the political life of Canada. Canada.

Robert Gourlay was born in Fife in 1778 midway between the American and French revolutions. The liberal ideas that produced both were topics of discussion in his home and in nearby St. Andrews University which he entered in 1793. A family friend was Sir James MacIntosh who wrote *Vindiciae Gallicae* in answer to Edmund Burke's attack on the "swinish multitude" in *Reflections on the Revolutions in France and on the proceedings in certain societies in London relative to that event*. Those debating societies, feared by the government for their radical political ideas, soon had branches in Scotland. When he was sixteen, Gourlay's father took him to Edinburgh to observe the trials of members of the Society of Friends of the People who were charged with treason. The contemporary interpretation of treason included inciting the people to agitate for electoral reform.

When he left the universities of St. Andrews and Edinburgh where he had studied the new subject of scientific agriculture, Gourlay set out on a grand tour of England, for the continent was closed to travel during the war with France. The year 1800 was a famine year in Britain, and what Gourlay saw of poverty in the agricultural districts convinced him that under the present system of government there could be no political and social justice for the common man. He had found his life's passion, and dedicated himself to improving the lot of the agricultural labourer. He returned to Scotland to live the life of a privileged young laird at Pratis, one of his father's five farms, and to make it a model of his social, economic and scientific convictions.

Gourlay soon became involved in the affairs of Fifeshire. In 1799, William Pitt had imposed an income tax to provide money for the war. As Gourlay pursued his voluntary duties as commissioner of supply, he listened to complaints about the regulations of the Income Tax Act. He was dissatisfied with parts of it himself, for the Act allowed no exemptions for capital expenditures for farm improvements. Gourlay, who was spending freely as he employed new methods of cultivation and watched over the well-being of his farm help, considered that his expenditures should be free from taxation since they helped to produce more food and lessen the possibility of famine. He wanted to discuss the terms of the Act at the meetings of the county heritors, a non-elective body that from time immemorial had administered the affairs of the county in the interests of the landowning class. At one of its meetings he rose to protest the fact that a discussion of the income tax was being postponed for a third time. He objected to this postponement, and in addition proposed that the heritors invite the tenant farmers to join in the discussion, for the income tax concerned them too. But landowners were not accustomed to consult their tenants. To invite them to a heritors' meeting was such a horrendous proposal that the chairman, the Earl of Kellie, leaped to his feet and, in the midst of the din that Gourlay's proposal aroused, he adjourned the meeting while Gourlay was still speaking.

To some writers the Earl's action has appeared as a good joke on a tiresome speaker. To Gourlay it was an arbitrary act on the part of a reactionary representative of a class tainted with the remnants of feudalism. Although it was treasonable to demand a widened franchise, he published two pamphlets, one protesting the rule of the antediluvians who dominated Fife and the other laying out a plan for parliamentary reform. The sheriff was instructed to seize them, and Gourlay would have been jailed or deported had he not moved to the south of England in 1809.

There he rented Deptford Farm, Wiltshire, from the Duke of Somerset who had been buying up farms in order to cash in on high wartime prices for grain. Gourlay proceeded to change the century-old pattern of the fields and farm buildings with great vigour, according to the latest scientific principles. His ploughmen and produce were soon carrying off prizes at the local fairs. His grain was among the first to reach market because he had purchased a new-fangled threshing machine. In addition, he paid his workers a living wage. The farm economy of the south of England was supported by the work of poorly paid seasonal labourers. In the winter, they were supposed to apply for parish relief. It was a system that was hated by the rich who were assessed to support people they said were too lazy to work; and it was hated by the poor who still retained enough pride to wish they could be self-supporting. Gourlay had not forgotten his vow to better the lot of the poor. But his living wage did not endear him to the neighbouring landowners who were forced to compete with him for labour.

Gourlay's success eventually proved to be his undoing. The man who had championed the tenant farmers of Fife was now a tenant himself, bound by an agreement whose terms he had not scrutinized too closely during his hasty exit from Fife. His agreement with the Duke of Somerset said that he was to assume payment of the poor rates assessed to the farm. In Scotland these rates had been minimal. In England he now found that they amounted to £100 yearly and, moreover he had to pay the tithe in kind. In Scotland most tithes had been commuted to cash, but now that Gourlay had increased the yield of his acres, the Duke asked for them in kind. Another problem arose over the rents Gourlay owed to the Duke. Gourlay had not been able to harvest a crop the first year for he had not had entry to the farm on the date specified. He insisted on his rights and refused to pay any rent until he had been compensated for losses incurred because the terms of his agreement had been breached. The Duke insisted on his rights, however, and served Gourlay with a notice of eviction in November, 1811, ordering the auction of Gourlay's goods to pay for the back rent.

If Gourlay submitted to the eviction and left the farm, he could receive no compensation for the large sums of money he had spent on improving the farm in preparation for the twenty-one years occupancy agreed upon. No other landowner would rent to an evicted tenant, and his family would be reduced to beggary. Arbitrary evictions of tenants were common enough at this time, but Robert Gourlay "refused to bow the knee to Haman" and retained Sir Samuel Romilly, a well-known liberal lawyer who had defended members of the Corresponding Societies. He sued the Duke and won his case with damages for not receiving entry to the farm at the time specified.

While he was waiting to receive this compensation, Gourlay wrote three pamphlets asking for reform of the poor laws and assisted the people of Wily parish to draw up two petitions. The first asked that a law be passed to prevent children under the age of twelve from being sent to work in the fields in order to qualify their parents for relief. The second asked for common land to be set aside in each parish so that the poor could grow their own food. Petitioning the king was an age-old custom, but in the era of Wellington and the Prince Regent petitioners were regarded as suspicious agitators. One government leader, Lord Sheffield (*Letter on the Corn Laws, 1815*) wrote: "Nothing, surely, is more disgusting than the new system of being instructed and governed by petitions from those who, from their stations in life, are the least informed, and perfectly incapable of judging their real, permanent interest." After a considerable effort to have the petitions laid before parliament, Gourlay at last succeeded, only to have them tabled indefinitely by the leader of the Whigs, Henry Brougham.

Gourlay had won his case against arbitrary eviction and had spoken out for the poor, but life for him and his family of five small children was now complicated by postwar depression and the bad harvest of the cold, wet year of 1816. On two occasions, however, he and his wife had been visited by Mrs. Gourlay's cousins from the Niagara District in Upper Canada. Both had prospered with seeming ease and both were now members of the provincial legislative council, the constitutional equivalent of the British House of Lords. The Honourable William Dickson and the Honourable Thomas Clark had urged him to give up tenant farming for a freer life in Canada, but at the time it had not seemed necessary to make the move. Now he was willing to entertain the idea. Part of Mrs. Gourlay's dowry had been 866 acres of land in Upper Canada. In 1800 when Mrs. Gourlay's uncle, the late Honourable Robert Hamilton, had given them to her, an acre of wild land was not worth sixpence; but now the land might mean a new life. In 1817 Robert Gourlay set sail for Canada to assess the potentiality of his land in Dereham township, Oxford County.

Gourlay's plans had always been ambitious and even as he crossed the ocean he was thinking of more than his own future. He was planning to compile and publish a statistical account of Upper Canada that would advertise its advantages to British emigrants so that they would choose to settle in Canada rather than the United States. He would send a questionnaire to the officials of every township to secure the necessary information. He had also studied the latest map of the province with a view to forming some idea of the best way to settle the poor of England in the new country to the advantage of both. If his own land were properly situated, he might use it for a beginning and, since his relatives Clark and Dickson owned about a township each, he probably had no doubt in his mind that he could obtain as much in order to implement his far-reaching aims for the poor.

Upper Canada was sparsely settled by a population of about 80,000. It had been formed by the United Empire Loyalists who had left the Thirteen Colonies during and after the American Revolution. The officials and the laws sent out from England to govern them had been accepted with few reservations for the new country was supposed to be a microcosm of the old and not of the revolutionary republic they had fled. Twenty-five years of existence had brought political differences to the fore, however, largely as the result of the unimpeded immigration of Americans into Upper Canada. The Loyalists had left the United States for reasons of loyalty. The newcomers were not similarly motivated and were not as inclined to accept the arbitrary powers wielded by the executive branch of government and its ally, the clergy of the Church of England. The Constitutional Act of 1791 had recognized the need for self-government, insofar as it had given them an elected assembly. But the officials of the appointed executive and legislative councils, Loyalists, for the most part, whose duty it was to accept or reject the recommendations of the assembly, were responsible for their actions, not to assembly, but to the Lieutenant-Governor and through him to the Colonial Office in Britain. The Colonial Secretary was Lord Bathurst who, till his death in 1834, would oppose parliamentary reform.

The members of the assembly, loyal though most of them were, were increasingly determined after 1815 to be an integral part of the government. By 1817 they had begun to pose embarrassing questions about money to their constitutional superiors, the executive and legislative councils. In 1816 they had voted £3000 for a gift of silver plate in gratitude for the services of Lieutenant-Governor Gore (who had been out of the province for the duration of the 1812-14 war) and £500 in gratitude for the services of retiring Chief Justice Scott. The ears of some of the candidates for re-election had been blistered in their home constituencies about the extravagance of the "Spoon Bill", and the assembly itself now wanted to know what was being done with the £2500 they had voted towards official salaries (the civil list) that was being "held in reserve" instead of being expended.

A newly elected assembly convened in February 1817. It was now determined to know what the executive government was going to do with the £8271 it had been asked to vote for the civil list in view of the fact that the previous £2500 had not been accounted for. A committee was appointed to find out. Ten days later Lieutenant-Governor Gore replied that he had the Prince Regent's command to pay retired Chief Justice Scott a pension of £800 sterling from it, and the remainder of the money was "subject to the disposition of His Majesty."

Not only was that answer unsatisfactory to the assembly, there were many other matters on which they wanted action. The 200-acre grants to the militia for war services had not been made and their pay was in arrears; war losses had not been compensated, though losses in neighbouring New York state had been settled long ago; the postal service was inefficient; the clergy and crown land reserves, designed to render church and state independent of control, were impediments in the way of settlers; Americans were being excluded from the province in accordance with a directive sent out by Lord Bathurst in 1815. When the assembly proceeded with extraordinary speed to approve resolutions dealing with the investigation of these matter, Lieutenant-Governor Gore prorogued it.

It was one of the ironies that governed Robert Gourlay's fate that he left England almost to the day on which Gore prorogued the legislature of Upper Canada. He arrived in Quebec on May 31, 1817, walked from Montreal to the new Perth settlement, where he prepared a statistical account of the settlement with a view to profiting from any mistakes that had been made in setting it up, and reached his relatives in the Niagara District at the end of the first week of July. He was bitten so badly by mosquitoes that he was ill in Thomas Clark's house for six weeks before he could undertake a trip to appraise his land in Dereham township.

When Gourlay's strength returned, he first took a walking tour of the Genessee District, as far as Albany. Exercise had always been his best medicine. Everywhere he travelled the roads were good and land was being sold, rather than given away, to put money in the public treasury. He returned to Upper Canada filled with enthusiasm for the future and an-

nounced to his relatives that he would go to the capital at York to ask permission to publicize his proposal for a statistical account of the province in the *Upper Canada Gazette*, the official newspaper. Both Dickson and Clark were in favour of a plan that would encourage immigrants who might buy the choice land they had for sale in Dumfries and Norfolk townships. Most officials in York proved to be enthusiastic too over a project that would bring prosperity to the province. They readily consented to the publication of Gourlay's questionnaire and the accompanying *Address to the Resident Land-owners of Upper Canada* that explained the project. He had little doubt that he would obtain the grant of land for which he applied, could collect the answers to the questionnaire and by December be on his way home to settle his affairs and bring out his family in the spring.

While he waited for an answer to his application for land, Gourlay decided to set out to view his land in Dereham township. The township meetings that were to provide answers to questions about the fertility of the soil and availability of roads, mills and minerals were beginning all over the province as he began his journey. There was no road into Dereham township and only one settler, and all along the way he was bombarded with questions about government land policy. He decided to continue to Sandwich at the western extremity of the province so that he would have complete knowledge of the land he was preparing to promote. He returned, confident that a grant of land would be waiting for him.

There was one official in York whom Gourlay had not asked for permission to distribute his questionnaire. He had not approached executive councillor, the Reverend John Strachan, for his Niagara relatives had described Strachan as anti-democratic, anti-American and rabidly in favour of an established Church of England. Dr. Strachan was piqued at being ignored. In addition, he knew before the thirty-first question was asked that the answers would be very similar to the resolutions put forward by the

Robert Gourlay, 1814   *By Permission of the Author*

John Strachan, First Anglican Bishop of Toronto   *Ontario Archives, Toronto*

prorogued assembly. He marked Gourlay as a revolutionary who would reinforce the dissidence already apparent in the province. This man must not be given land that would encourage him to remain. On January 6, 1818, the clerk of the executive council despatched a letter refusing Gourlay's application for land.

Gourlay had listened to complaints of others all the way to Sandwich and back. Now he had one of his own. He wrote a letter to the editor of the *Niagara Spectator* saying that the development of Upper Canada and the welfare of thousands of people in Britain would be influenced adversely by the rejection. He was no man to give in lightly for by now his plans were known across the province and he had received reports from forty townships. These corroborated the general opinion that the Land Council's policy was to keep the best land for favourites and to send settlers out at random locations far from roads and markets. Many also resented the fact that Lieutenant-Governor Simcoe's proclamation inviting Americans to emigrate to Canada had been set aside after the War of 1812. No report at all came from the Home District around York. York was the capital from which ex-dominie Strachan had written only a few months before: "In the Lower House I shall by means of my pupils three of whom are already there possess a growing influence such as no other person can possess . . . "[1] And now the news came to Gourlay that some of his reports had been taken illegally out of the Kingston post office after Strachan's recent visit to Cornwall.

While Strachan had been conferring with his friends about the danger posed by this newcomer to the province, Gourlay was listening again to his Niagara relatives. January was the month when Americans often came to buy land, but no strange sleigh bells jingled in this year because of imperial land and immigration policy. On January 10, 1815, Lord Bathurst had issued a directive restricting the entry of Americans for fear they would alienate Canada from Britain. In October Lieutenant-Governor Gore, with the approval of the executive council, instructed the commissioners not to administer the oath of allegiance to immigrants without special consent.[2] Dickson claimed that this order had not been approved by the legislature, and he continued to do so until he was relieved of his status as commissioner.

Now that the government was at an impasse and business was stagnating, Dickson told Gourlay, the conduct of the government was sufficient to justify rebellion. One night when Dickson had drunk too many toasts at a dinner of the regiment of which he was colonel, he asserted loudly that if things did not change he would rather live under the American flag than the British. All this, the sixty township reports now in his hands, and the fact that parliament was about to convene for the first regular annual session since its prorogation the previous May, caused Gourlay to issue a second *Address to the Resident Landowners of Upper Canada*. He pointed out that the parliament of Upper Canada must beware or it would become "the tool, if not the sport, of executive power." He read it to William Dickson who roared his approval, slapped him on the back, and offered him 500 acres of land for reminding the assembly to insist on its rights. Dickson approved the resolutions of the assembly that had caused it to be prorogued, particularly the one requesting the admission of Americans who were his best customers. Dickson's favourite toast, when draining a glass of wine, was: "There goes another acre of land!"[3]

After this show of approbation, Gourlay jumped on his horse and rode off to show the *Address* to magistrate Samuel Street, a business partner of Thomas Clark's. When Street read it, he trembled. Gourlay was asking for a British parliamentary inquiry into the government of Upper Canada. He asked the people to deluge parliament with petitions for redress of the present system under which soured settlers were returning to the United States. Street feared the *Address* might be termed seditious, and he pulled out a copy of the Seditious Alien Act of 1804 that had been passed to keep French and Irish republicans from entering Canada from the United States. Gourlay read it and laughed. He said he was no alien; he was a British subject and the Act could not be applied to him. He rode off to the office of the *Niagara Spectator* and gave the editor his second *Address* to print.

Before the paper came off the press legislative councillors Dickson and Clark departed for York for the opening of the legislature. When Gourlay received a copy of the Speech from the Throne and found that it was filled with platitudes instead of recommendations that would answer the known needs of the province, he published all his correspondence with York about his request for land. Then he abandoned the reasonable tone of his two *Addresses*. What was wrong with York, he asked? The conduct of public affairs at little York was "dull, dirty and disgusting. . . . "You have lost yourself in some horrid Stygian shade where the souls of you have been sucked out by the thirsty vampire, or does the Land Council labour under a night-mare. Has it devoured too much land and gone to sleep while the crude mass is yet undigested? . . . How is it that it has duties to perform and cannot perform them?"[4] The first act of a government that said it had no money, he advised Administrator Smith, should be to tax wild land held by speculators or borrow from Lloyd's of London. The great want of the province was "ready service on the part of the Land Council, and land in situations where it was possible to clear it." As for Dr. Strachan, Gourlay offered to "clear the church of cobwebs within: perhaps, I might fit it with a steeple and a bell, and make it look decent beside the *palace* of its pastor." He also claimed that Strachan had been preparing to write a book about Upper Canada and that he had stolen Strachan's thunder; hence Strachan's animosity towards him.

The columns of Upper Canada's little papers soon were smoking with letters for and against Gourlay. Many were pleased with the turmoil that promised to stir the government to action, but Thomas Clark was aghast at what he believed was a breach of good manners on Gourlay's part. He wrote Gourlay from York begging him to leave the province by way of Sackett's Harbour, New York; but Gourlay's work was not yet done. Neither was the work of the assembly. Again it was fighting for recognition against the power of the two appointed councils. It brought in a bill to tax the land of the absentees, and when it was asked to approve a further £12,603 for the year's civil list, it passed a bill rescinding the £2500 voted in 1816 and still unaccounted for. The legislative councillors were kept busy returning money bills that the assembly claimed it had the power to initiate. Strachan wrote superciliously to the secretary of the governor-in-chief in Quebec that the fight was only a little dispute about interfering in money bills. Acting Administrator Smith wrote to Lord Bathurst for advice. For its part, the assembly was no backwoods aggregation. It knew that it was engaged in a struggle over the power of the purse and if it did not possess it, it might as well not exist. A petition was prepared to be sent to the Prince Regent over the heads of the councils. Smith refused to submit it. By now he was at a loss what to do. Taking the line of least resist-ance, he prorogued the legislature, April 1, 1818.

"The fools," said Robert Gourlay when the news reached him, "were dismissed on their own proper day," and he sat down to write a Third *Address to the Resident Landowners of Upper Canada.* "Gentlemen, Your Parliament is broken up! . . . For three years the laws have been thwarted, and set aside by executive power; . . . " If parliament was not to be allowed to petition the Prince Regent, then the people must do it directly. They must meet in every township to elect representatives to draft a petition to the Prince Regent that would be discussed at a Convention to be held in York in July. Every supporter should pay a dollar towards the expenses of a commission to convey it to London. With proper government Upper Canada could become the most flourishing and habitable spot on the globe.

Dickson, Clark and 900 others in the Niagara District subscribed their dollars and once again, like wildfire, meetings sprang up all over the province. The Niagara District drafted a petition and printed one thousand copies of a pamphlet called *Principles and Proceedings of the Inhabitants of the District of Niagara for addressing his Royal Highness the Prince Regent.* The book and the meetings were soon labelled as seditious by the authorities, for it appeared that the proposed Convention might usurp the powers of the legal government, just as a Convention in France had done not too long before. York officials sought to prevent the meetings. They declared that the common people had no right to petition the throne. When Gourlay journeyed to the Midland District to organize meetings, he was physically assaulted for objecting to the removal of his township reports from the post office. When Gourlay pasted up placards announcing times of the meetings Philip Vankoughnett, former pupil of Strachan's in loyalist Cornwall, newly elected member of the assembly and violent anti-American, clattered after him in a wagon and pulled them down. They burned Gourlay's books in Cornwall. They arrested him in Kingston on a charge of seditious libel, and a second time in Cornwall. Supporters supplied him with bail. John Beverley Robinson, attorney-general, was ordered to find a way to declare the meetings illegal. He searched the statutes as far back as the time of Charles II but could find no precedent.

The Convention of Friends to Inquiry was held in York in July. Despite the fears of the government there was no violence, only a peaceful resolve to delay sending the petition to London until the delegates assessed the actions of the newly appointed lieutenant-governor, Sir Peregrine Maitland, who was due to arrive early in the fall. Meanwhile, Gourlay had still to face two charges of seditious libel. Because he had followed all the "freedom trials" in Scotland and England, he intended to conduct his own defence. At Kingston the Crown sought to convict him of libel on the basis of words taken from the draft petition to the Prince Regent: "The lands of the Crown in Upper Canada are of immense extent . . . . The disposal of this land is left to Ministers at home, who are palpably ignorant of existing circumstances; and to a council of men resident in the province, who, it is believed, have long converted the trust reposed in them to purposes of selfishness . . . ." At Cornwall a passage was chosen from the third address: " . . . . For three years the laws have been thwarted, and set aside by executive power; — for three sessions have your legislators sat in Assembly, and given sanction to the monstrous, — the hideous abuse . . . ." Gourlay argued his cases brilliantly. Neither jury would convict him for saying what concurred with their own views. Henry John Boulton, acting solicitor-general, departed ignominiously while the rafters rang with shouts of "Gourlay Forever". Gourlay had been declared a free and loyal man. He departed for New York via Boston to pick up his mail from home, intending to return to Upper Canada to solicit the patronage of Sir Peregrine for the statistical account of Upper Canada that he had promised to publish.

When Sir Peregrine Maitland arrived in Upper Canada he was anxious to govern well, but he was an ex-soldier appointed by a Tory administration unsympathetic to political liberalism. He convened parliament in October, for the treasury was empty, and immediately asked for a law to declare illegal the meetings that were being held to continue the watchdog work of the Convention of the Friends to Inquiry. Upper Canada had its Gagging Act as well as Britain, and the assembly, anxious to demonstrate its loyalty to a new Governor, not only complied but expunged from its own minutes all references to the recent struggle. This infuriated Gourlay. Where was the power of the Commons now, he jibed in the *Niagara Spectator*, whose editor was arrested for publishing his letter. Again Gourlay called meetings, though under different names from that designated in the Act to Prevent Certain Meetings. Meanwhile, petitions poured in to the government deploring the continued persecution of a man who had twice been acquitted of seditious libel. The Tories dismissed them by saying that they were the work of school children. But clearly it was time to be rid of this gadfly.

Chief Justice Powell was asked to reinterpret the Seditious Alien Act of 1804. The word he seized on was the word "inhabitant." For the purpose of this Act, an alien, as opposed to an inhabitant, was one who had not taken the oath of allegiance and who had been absent in a foreign country, leaving no fixed residence behind him, during the last six months. This interpretation would exempt from prosecution the Chief Justice himself who had departed for Boston on the same lake boat as Gourlay, but who had a fixed residence. Gourlay had only land; he had not taken the oath of allegiance in Upper Canada, for it was required only when acquiring land or opening a business; and he had gone to New York within the last six months to pick up letters from his wife. William Dickson, now in danger of dismissal from his position as legislative councillor if he countenanced his relative further, was induced to ask his neighbour Isaac Swayze, a zealous government supporter, to swear that Robert Gourlay had not been an inhabitant of Upper Canada for the preceding six months. Gourlay was served with a warrant ordering him to leave the province in three days or be hanged, drawn and quartered according to the medieval penalty designated in the Seditious Alien Act. Gourlay refused to submit to an order that implied he was a danger to the province. He had never countenanced violence, only petitioning; and had twice been acquitted of the charge of sedition. If he left without a fair trial the liberty of all individuals was endangered. He refused to leave, and was taken to the jail on the outskirts of what is now Niagara-on-the-Lake to await trial in the next assizes in August.

When the time came for his trial Gourlay was so weakened by confinement in a closed cell during the hottest summer the province had ever known, and so bewildered by his efforts to discover the charge he was to face — he could never believe that it was failure to leave the province when ordered — that his defence was feeble and confused. On August 20, 1819, a jury declared him guilty of not leaving the province when ordered by two legislative councillors. The sentence was banishment on pain of death if he returned. Chief Justice Powell advised him, in passing sentence, to put his great talents to better use than he had done. Meanwhile, the patriots who were responsible for ridding the country of this menace quietly removed from the minute-books of the courts of Midland and Niagara districts the records of Gourlay's trials.

In the election of 1820, all four of Gourlay's opponents in the Niagara District were defeated and four of Gourlay's supporters (plus four others across the province) were elected in their places. But Gourlay himself was gone, back to Britain. In 1822 he published a two-volume *Statistical Account of Upper Canada*, the basis of much of our present knowledge of the province at the time. Gourlay also renewed his efforts to call attention to the need for an inquiry into the state of affairs in Upper Canada. On one occasion, he administered a

GENERAL INTRODUCTION

TO

STATISTICAL ACCOUNT

OF

Upper Canada,

COMPILED

WITH A VIEW TO A GRAND SYSTEM

OF

EMIGRATION,

IN CONNEXION WITH A REFORM OF THE

POOR LAWS.

BY ROBERT GOURLAY.

" Thy spirit, Independence, let me share,
" Lord of the lion-heart and eagle-eye!"

London:
PUBLISHED BY SIMPKIN AND MARSHALL, STATIONERS' COURT, AND J. M. RICHARDSON, CORNHILL.

1822.

Title page of Gourlay's *Statistical Account*

Courtesy of Mills Memorial Library, McMaster University

few smart taps with a riding crop on Henry Brougham's shoulder in the lobby of the House of Commons. Brougham was still ignoring petitions. For this Gourlay was imprisoned in Coldbath Fields along with other "insane" political prisoners. While he was imprisoned, the Upper Canadian government put the Crown lands up for sale, and John Galt, the real estate promoter who sold them, used part of the *Statistical Account* as promotion material.

In 1837, when the rebellion against the Family Compact broke out under William Lyon Mackenzie, Gourlay refused to support it. He still would not condone violence as a means of achieving changes. In 1842 the legislature of the United Province of Canada revoked the sentence of banishment and Gourlay was free to occupy his land in Oxford County. He could still charm people when he was eighty. In 1858 James MacIntyre, the "Cheese Poet" of Oxford County, described him:

> There came to Oxford Robert Gourlay
> In his old age his health was poorly . . .
> Yet he was erect and tall
> Like noble, ruined castle wall . . . .

Was Gourlay foolish or inspired? Were the men who prosecuted him wrong and was he alone right? They were truly convinced they were right; Gourlay less so. In 1843 he wrote, a little wistfully, in his diary that he was a stone that the Builder had rejected. Yet it was Robert Gourlay, one of the neglected men of Canadian history, who published the first book in Upper Canada; who made the first political tour of the province; who founded the first political party, Gourlayism, a name in use till 1850; who was the first Canadian to be banished for political opinions; who published the first *Statistical Account of Upper Canada*; who first called the mother country to inquire into the state of affairs in Upper Canada; and whose sensible recommendations for a better immigration policy influenced Edward Gibbon Wakefield, one of the commissioners who accompanied Lord Durham to Canada after the rebellion and who designed the emigration policies on which the settlement of Australia was based. If that commission of investigation had been sent when Robert Gourlay suggested it years before, the rebellion of 1837 might not have been necessary.

Footnotes

1. John Strachan to the Lord Bishop of Quebec (in England), 12 May 1817, reprinted in *The John Strachan Letter Book*, ed. George Spragge (Toronto, 1946), p. 165.

2. Public Archives of Canada, Upper Canada Sundries, Minutes of the Executive Council, 7 Oct. 1815; Robert Gourlay, *Statistical Account of Upper Canada*, II (2 vols., London, 1822), pp. 416, 427.

3. *Ibid.*, p. 493.

4. Robert Gourlay, *The Banished Briton and Neptunian*, #19 (Boston, 1843), pp. 211, 214.

Note on Sources

The research on which this article is based draws heavily upon Gourlay's widely scattered publications, and upon documents contained in the Melville Correspondence (National Library, Edinburgh), the Liverpool Letterbook (British Museum), the Macaulay Papers (Public Archives of Ontario), the Powell Papers (Metropolitan Toronto Central Library), and the Upper Canada Sundries (Public Archives of Canada). More extensive documentation is presented in the author's recent book, *Robert Gourlay, Gadfly* (44 Uplands Ave., Thornhill: The Ampersand Press, 1971).

Across The Rockies and The Selkirks with G.M. Grant in 1883
P.B. Waite

Rev. George Monro Grant
Queen's University Archives, Kingston, Ontario

George Monro Grant was born in 1835 at Albion Mines, Nova Scotia, the third child of James Grant and Mary Monro. Both parents had come to Pictou County from Scotland in the 1820's. Young Grant was educated at Pictou Academy and in 1853 was sent by the Pictou Synod, with three other young men, to Glasgow University to study for the ministry in the Presbyterian church. Grant was an excellent student, hard-working, quick, and intelligent, and he had withal a restless, fresh, colonial energy that attracted students and professors alike. A reply of his in a student debate at Glasgow is typical. A student had referred contemptuously to a Conservative association. "There's no such thing," Grant thundered, "it's a club." "What's the difference?" asked the student. "There's an association, gentlemen," said Grant flinging out his left hand, the fingers hanging limp and separate; "and there's a club," and at the word club his closed fist shot out straight from the shoulder, the whole effect eloquent of the utter difference between limp separateness and the smashing power of united force.[1]

Grant was ordained in December, 1860 as missionary for Nova Scotia, and he returned there in January, 1861. His first work was at River John, about 15 miles west of Pictou, whence he was transferred to Prince Edward Island. One local elder was for a time suspicious of him as an import from the old land. The two went for a walk early in winter and Grant stepped so fearlessly and familiarly over the icy road that the elder said with pleasure, "Ye canna be a Scotchman; nae Scotchman walks on ice that way." "Oh, no," said Grant, "I'm from Pictou." That was all that was necessary.[2]

In 1862, when he was 27, Grant was asked to become minister at St. Matthews Church, Halifax, the largest and perhaps the most influential Presbyterian church in Nova Scotia, whose foundation went back to 1750. The new church that Grant came to in 1863 was built in 1857-58, and still stands in Barrington Street. Grant was not a sanctimonious or even an ascetic minister; he loved life, hated hypocrisy, had no patience with what he considered pious anachronisms in the church. An organ was installed in St. Matthews after ten years' uphill work. It was the same with sabbatarianism. He opposed Sunday streetcars in Halifax where he felt they were not needed, but later supported them in Montreal and Toronto where they were. He was an ardent supporter of Confederation; in this, as in a number of other issues (and attitudes) he and the Irish Roman Catholic Archbishop of Halifax, Thomas Connolly, got along well together. Their churches were not more than a hundred yards apart, and they admired and trusted each other.

Grant went to Queen's University in 1877, as Principal. He did a great deal for Queen's in the years to come, and died in harness in 1902. From the very beginning — as he had always done — he set about strengthening Queen's financial foundation. Hard and distasteful work it was that campaign in 1878 — or at any other time, as university presidents know. Grant did not have a soft nature; he had a temper which occasionally showed itself. In Kingston he visited one man whose ample means were equalled by his avariciousness, peculiarly unpleasant to Grant as it was glossed over by an unctuous piety. "Mr. Smith," said Grant, "can you not give something for the college?" Mr. Smith protested his interest, his desire, but added the hard times, his liberality elsewhere, etc. So much had he given in fact that he said to Grant, "Really, Principal Grant, considering the claims upon me, I should be committing a sin if I gave any more." "Mr. Smith," Grant's voice was intense and hard, "that is a lie black enough to sink a whole shipload of souls."[3]

Grant had been at Glasgow with James Bryce, whom he in some ways resembled, and not only in appearance. Never ready to suffer fools, perhaps rather cocksure of himself, but blessed with rugged good health and daemonic energy, Grant was a natural outdoorsman, much as Bryce was. Grant also had a sage, earthy good sense about him, a rugged honesty, and a refreshing candour. He was a good man to have with you on a walk, a hike, or an expedition, determined, capable and fearless. On the hazardous trail down the Kicking Horse River Grant admits "we did not like it."[4] His companion, Sandford Fleming, no novice himself in the mountains, was much more uncomfortable:

> A series of precipices run sheer up from the boiling current to form a contracted canyon. A path has therefore been traced along the hill side, ascending to the election of some seven or eight hundred feet. For a long distance not a vestige of vegetation is to be seen. On the steep acclivity our line of advance is narrow, so narrow that there is scarcely a foothold . . . .
> We cross clay, rock and gravel slides at a giddy height. To look down gives one an uncontrollable dizziness, to make the head swim . . . . I do not think that I can ever forget that terrible walk; it was the greatest trial I ever experienced.[5]

Grant had met Fleming in Halifax in the 1860's. Fleming first appeared there in connection with the Intercolonial surveys that began in 1863, and he took up summer residence in Halifax, on the North West Arm, indeed died there in 1915. They were both physically active men, both possessed of a driving curiosity about the world, and tough enough to set about exploring it. Their best known trek together was in 1872, when Fleming was 45, Grant 37, crossing Canada from *Ocean to Ocean*, the title in fact of the book Grant published in 1873. They made their way by train and boat to Thunder Bay, canoed to Fort Garry, crossed the prairie on horseback, and by horse and foot over the Yellowhead Pass and down to the Pacific by the North Thompson and the Fraser River. They left Halifax July 1st: they were at New Westminster on October 4th, 1872.

Eleven years later, in 1883, the two men made another great western trek. It may need saying that both men were also eleven years older as well, and for Fleming, at age 56, it was a considerable feat. In June, 1883 Fleming had been in England on business when he was cabled by George Stephen, President of the Canadian Pacific Railway, asking if Fleming would travel west and look over the Kicking Horse-Rogers Pass proposed route and at the same time inspect the section between Kamloops and Port Moody that was being constructed by the Canadian Government. This last section had been contracted for by the Macdonald government before the C.P.R. contract was signed; but it was put in the contract that when completed that section was to be given over to the C.P.R. Stephen had a strong suspicion that this government section was not being built to C.P.R. standard, even though the Government said it was. Stephen's view, and that of a number of others, was that given the enormous difficulties of the work, especially in the Fraser Canyon, the Government and its contractor, Andrew Onderdonk, had been skimping on specifications. Fleming was in fact later to confirm this. There was subsequently a protracted arbitration over that section.

Fleming wrote Grant, asking him if he would like to come, and it was agreed they would meet first in Halifax, and then rendezvous in Winnipeg. Fleming had to see Stephen and the rest of the C.P.R. Board of Directors in Montreal, and in Toronto pick up his son, Sandford Hall Fleming, who was coming with him. The idea was to travel as far as the C.P.R. would take them, that is, to Calgary, and then, depending upon the information available to them there, would try to get through to Kamloops by the Kicking Horse and Rogers Passes.

Grant made his way by train and steamer to Port Arthur, thence to Kenora by canoe, and by the new railway to Winnipeg. Their baggage and equipment supplied in part by the Hudson's Bay Company (no doubt much of it at C.P.R. expense), the whole party left Winnipeg on Monday morning, August 20, 1883, by C.P.R. train. They travelled in style; Stephen had seen to that.

> Our private car is a most luxurious one; consisting of dining room large bedroom, and sitting room furnished with four magnificent arm chairs, & ten sofas that can be made into beds.

The C.P.R. route taken by Grant in 1883

During that first day they invited Archbishop Taché, and George Stephen's brother, also travelling westward, to lunch, finishing off with peach tart, fresh fruit, and lager.[6] Grant seems never to have been a teetotaler. They arrived in Calgary Wednesday evening, August 22, and at noon next day were on their way by waggon to Morley. By Sunday, August 26 they were at what is now Banff, Grant, Fleming, and others by this time on horseback. (At the summit, all their provisions and impedimenta were put onto five packhorses.) They camped that Sunday night below Castle Mountain (now, and regrettably, called Mount Eisenhower), slept on spruce and pine boughs over which a buffalo robe was thrown and snuggled down under two or three blankets. It was already cold at night; the water in the basin outside was frozen the next day. Grant wrote to his wife after breakfast, on a glorious Monday morning:

> . . . we have just had a good breakfast of porridge and condensed milk, bacon & bread & corn [?], & dried apples cooked nicely. The waggon with our dunnage got away at 6.45; & we are to follow in half an hour. Everything is going on nicely. Everyone we meet, even the roughest teamsters, civil & obliging; the air & water first class, & at every point the scenery simply superb, finer in my opinion than the Alps because of the infinite multiplicity & finish of detail, as if these mighty masses had been piled up by masons & then chiselled & sculptured by artists.[7]

By Sunday, September 2, after a ferocious, indeed hair-raising, trail down the Kicking Horse River they reached the Columbia; the following Sunday they were camped wet and miserable on the western slope of the Selkirks, along the Ille-cille-waet River. It was one of the most difficult parts of their journey, though they had no easy time either through Eagle Pass — through the Gold Range — which was still without a trail. The worst was the devil's club (*Panax horridus*) whose fierce pricks left festering wounds; but almost as bad was the skunk cabbage (*Pothos foetidus*) the Latin name of which conveys more of its character than the English. Of deadfalls, and thick, wet undergrowth, there seemed no end, nor was there a trail. The west slopes of the Selkirks rejoice in an annual precipitation of about sixty inches and it rains or snows nearly two hundred days a year.

But at last they arrived at Shuswap Lake, Sunday September 16, and picked up a waiting steamer to Kamloops. "I feel as strong as ever I did," Grant wrote his wife the next day, "though the hardships were real. My hand[s] were cut and jagged in an awful way. On my left [half of Grant's right was missing as the result of a childhood mishap] I counted the other day 33 gashes, cuts scratches [?] & festering sores . . . ."[8] Grant and Fleming reached Victoria at the end of September, and Grant was to rejoin his wife at Winnipeg, travelling by the Northern Pacific, on Saturday, October 6.

Fleming wrote up the story of this trip, as Grant had the 1872 one, and published it in Montreal the next year: *England and Canada: a summer tour between Old and New Westminster with historical notes*. Fleming was not, however, a great writer; nor had he any touch of the poet. He is laconic, sturdy and honest, letting the story tell itself. Grant, on the other hand, was much more impressionable and spirited; he was clearly taken, at times overwhelmed, with the sheer grandeur of the country. His account of the trip was published in a series of articles in *The Week*, an excellent magazine of political and literary comment, that was begun in Toronto by Goldwin Smith in 1883. Aside from a brief mention in W. L. Grant's book about his father, *Principal Grant*, in 1904, the articles have largely disappeared from sight. They seem just too good to pass up, and they are reprinted, in a somewhat abridged form, here. There were eleven articles, about 2500 words each, running altogether to about 30,000 words. They appeared first in *The Week* of December 18, 1883, and ran more or less regularly until May 22, 1884. They are based largely on Grant's journal and upon the letters he sent so assiduously to his wife whenever there was opportunity. Both originals are written in pencil, more often than not, sitting around camp after a hard morning or afternoon's travel. There are few dates in Grant's published account. Dates have been inserted in square brackets through the narrative.

Grant was a great wanderer. He confessed as much writing to his wife after their fourteenth wedding anniversary, apologizing for having forgotten it (his wife had had to remind him, like many another husband), and for his perennial travels, and telling her, solicitous and sensible husband that he was, that he thanked God for giving him "such a true sweet wise wife," and how their fourteen years together had seemed but a few days.[9] Their years were to end in 1901 with her death. Grant, his mighty constitution laid low by kidney disease, died in May, 1902. It was entirely characteristic of him that his last words were, "Get it done quickly." His brother remarked to Grant's son, on hearing the news, that Grant's dying was just like him: "the two notes of his character — action and promptitude: Something to be done and no dawdling in the doing of it."[10]

The C.P.R., By The Kicking Horse Pass And The Selkirks*
by
George M. Grant

I. Introductory

Is our North-West a reality or is it not? was the question that eleven or twelve years ago often engaged my thoughts. The Maritime and Inland Provinces had been Confederated. The Hudson Bay Company had sold out, and British Columbia had united itself to the Dominion. But could this half-continent of ours be bound into the material unity that is indispensable to the formation of national life? The difficulties in the way were enough to frighten dreamers, not to speak of sober politicians. The Inter-Colonial Railway was not constructed, and commercial authorities asserted that when it was there would not be traffic enough to buy

*The text as reprinted here contains the misspellings and misnomers of the original, e.g., Calgarry for Calgary; Ille-cille-want for Illecillewaet.

grease for the wheels. On every map of the trackless wilderness that extended from the Ottawa to the Red River of the North were written the words "impracticable for Railways." The testimonies about the North-West itself were so contradictory that no one knew what to believe. A writer in the *Edinburgh Review* had proved that it was out of the question to raise cereals, except, perhaps, at a few favoured points, on such a soil, and in such a climate. The testimony of an Archbishop who lived long in the country was to the same effect. A popular statesman called it a frozen wilderness of God knows what, extending God knows where . . . . If all or half of those things were so, then what was the use of our struggling to be a nation? Difficulties may be overcome but to fight against impossibilities is folly. Longing to be satisfied, I embraced an opportunity that was offered [in 1872] and after travelling across the country from the Atlantic to the Pacific, I came to the conclusion that the problem was one of difficulty, not of impossibility.

Since that time many things have happened. The Intercolonial Railway has been built and pays for its grease. No one now dreams of travelling from Central Canada to the Maritime Provinces by any other route . . . . Farther, a route was located between the Red River and the Pacific Coast, running through the acknowledged "fertile belt" to the foot of the Rocky Mountains, and thence through passes so favourable that the heaviest grade was fifty-two feet to the mile, and that only in one place and for a short distance. The most difficult section was the end nearest the Pacific, and that had been put under contract when Port Moody was adopted as the terminus. No other transcontinental railway built or projected could show anything like such a profile as the Canada Pacific.

Difficulties that few of us have any conception of had been overcome. But the people generally did not think of what had been accomplished. They thought only of the delays which they did not understand, of the great expenditure that had been incurred, of the indefinitely greater expenditure that was threatened, and of the charges of jobbery, corruption and incapacity that filled the air and poisoned their minds. They were becoming impatient of the burden. And who can wonder? Never before had three or four millions of comparatively poor people undertaken so gigantic a public work. Cries were heard to which politicians could not be deaf. The railway must be built by a company. We want to know how much this railway is going to cost. Better accede to any terms than go it blind any longer. Far better, it was even muttered, to give a company all the land in the North-West on condition of its building the railway, than remain longer in suspense, and in peril, for aught we know, of national bankruptcy. That this was the prevailing sentiment the representatives of the people well knew; and therefore no voice was raised, in the only place from which a voice can be heard over the whole land, in favour of the Government continuing to prosecute the work. That being the case, whenever a company with sufficient financial strength had contracted with the Government to build the road, criticism of the details of the bargain was little better than shooting arrows in the air. But let us clearly understand, a more emphatic condemnation of our party system cannot be conceived than this universal confession that no Government could be trusted with the prosecution of the one public work essential to national development, a work so vast, relatively to the country as a whole, that any one who gave an hour's thought to the subject must have seen that the company to which it was handed over would of necessity be a power stronger than any Government. Ordinarily, the relation between contractors and a Government is perfectly well understood. Both parties know which is the stronger. But when the work is of such a magnitude that the failure of the company would paralyze the whole country, the Government dare not let the company fail. It must put it beyond the possibility of failing. It must give it good terms to begin with, and must back it up to the end . . . .

The line recommended by Mr. Fleming for the C.P.R. ran northwesterly from the Red River through the "Fertile Belt," as Captain Palliser called it, that borders the North Saskatchewan. This was the arch or rainbow of good land round the semi-desert region that was said to project itself into Canada from the Great American Desert to the south; "a continuous belt, rich in water, woods and pasturage," that almost all previous explorers had united in praising. Such a route, of course, avoided the supposed semi-desert that a line running due west would have to cross. It had other advantages. The terminus on the Pacific coast could not be decided at once, and it was necessary to adopt a pass through the Rocky Mountains, which would be equally convenient for any of the harbours proposed. The Yellow Head was such a good common point, besides being a much better pass than those to the south, and being also so far north that the Selkirk range — across which no pass, up to that time, had been found — was completely flanked and avoided altogether. Other things being equal, it was well, too, that a national line should run through the heart of the North-West, all the more so when the boundless Peace

River prairies — a new North-West in themselves — were taken into account. Branches could be built to the main trunk from the north or the south, and thus in the end a regular herring-bone system of railways be established instead of the chaotic no-system that results from lack of plan or foresight. However, at the time when the company or Syndicate took the great work out of the hands of the Government, the former aspect of things had changed to a considerable extent. Port Moody had been selected as the Pacific terminus, and, therefore, a line as directly west from Winnipeg as possible would be decidedly the shortest. Not only so, but Mr. John Macoun, now Dominion Botanist, had been sent out, at Mr. Fleming's urgent and repeated request, to explore the country west and south from Winnipeg to the Mountains,[11] and he had reported that the land was infinitely better than had been supposed. Evidently Captain Palliser must have visited it after two or three exceptionally dry seasons.[12] Mr. Macoun declared the whole valley of the Qu'Appelle better for farming purposes than Manitoba, and found nothing but good soil on the immense treeless expanse of the Souris plain north-westward to Moose Jaw, which the old explorers had pronounced semi-desert. The experience of settlers who have gone to both districts during the last two or three years has proved that Mr. Macoun was right, though at the time he was derided as a mere enthusiast. Even west of the Coteau of the Missouri he found nutritious grasses and excellent pastures everywhere, with a very small percentage of bad land. In a word, it seems that the Syndicate considered that they had sufficient reasons to change the north-westerly to a westerly route that would make their line the shortest of all Trans-Continental Railways. Of course, I assume that when they came to such a decision, their engineers had asserted that there would be no insuperable difficulties in crossing the three ranges of mountains that interposed between the plains and their objective point. For, now-a-days, engineers laugh at difficulties. Double engines can be stationed at the heavy grades, tunnels cut by the dozen and any obstacle overcome, if only there is money enough.

There is no need to refer to the energy displayed by the Syndicate from the day when the work was committed to their hands. The most sanguine railway man would have smiled significantly, had he been told that in the summer of 1883 the line would be at Calgarry, and the run of 840 miles from Winnipeg to the Rocky Mountains made in thirty-six hours. The combination of qualities that effected this phenomenal result, the forethought on the part of the heads and the discipline of the whole force are simply beyond praise.

But, notwithstanding their uninterrupted and brilliant success, I heard mutterings when in Winnipeg last July to the effect that a great mistake had been made in changing the route. Of course the boom in Manitoba had collapsed, and the loudest talkers of two years ago were meek, not to say depressed with regard to everything under the sun. But people who seemed to know were heard alleging that the good land ceased at Regina or Moose Jaw; that the Kicking Horse Pass was impracticable; and that no pass had yet been discovered across the Selkirks. If any one of those assertions should turn out to be a fact, it would be decidedly unfortunate. Anxious to know the truth on the subject I determined to see the country for myself, as far as the end of the track at any rate; and when Mr. Fleming wrote me in August[13] that he intended to go not only to the end of the track, but to attempt to push on thence over the whole of the proposed route to the Pacific, and invited me to accompany him, I accepted the offer as readily as I had accepted his offer eleven years previously to travel with him across Canada from ocean to ocean.

Of the journey to Winnipeg nothing need be said, except to express wonder that any one would go by rail in summer when he can go by the lakes from Sarnia, Collingwood, Owen Sound, or — next year — Algoma Mills. Our party met in Winnipeg on the 18th of August, and after getting an outfit for the journey at the H.B. store, we started on the 20th.

II. On the Road to Calgarry

Across the plains and prairies for 840 miles, what a distance it seemed eleven years ago, and what possibilities were involved in the journey. Though our path was to be through the heart of "the fertile belt," as much thought was required in arranging an outfit as if we had intended to cross the Sahara . . . . The only oases we could look forward to were the H. B. forts, three or four hundred miles apart. And once on the trail, forty miles a day was considered very good travelling.

Last August, we stepped on board a car at the Winnipeg station on Monday morning, and on Wednesday night we slept in Calgarry.

Of course, the modern style of doing the North-West is very satisfactory to those whose supreme object in travelling is to get over the ground. And, as we were anxious to get into the mountains as soon as possible so as to get to the other side of them before winter, we did not grumble at railway speed. But everyone missed the joys of the old style; the glorious rides across the interminable plains, down into the widely eroded valleys that the smallest streams make, up and down the picturesque slopes of the Touchwood Hills, and along the far-extending banks of the North Saskatchewan; jogging quietly on for hours, after or before the carts, and turning aside only when our botanist called us to look at a new flower or plant; bursting into full gallop, shouting like school-boys out for a holiday, and as we rode far ahead — buoyed up with the excitement arising from the feeling that everything was new and that there was no knowing what we might see at any moment; perhaps, bringing down a prairie hen that rose from the thick grass so close to our feet that it seemed a shame to shoot; or hitting a duck on one of the innumerable lakelets that dot the face of the country, and getting mired in vain attempts to secure it, each man then upbraiding his fellow for not bringing a dog as part of the outfit; one day chasing a shambling but most nimble bear through brushwood, and the next excited by signs — that proved fallacious — of a herd of buffalo; camping beside glistening lakes or on velvety prairie, where we slept literally on roses; stimulated from morning to night by an atmosphere the purest, sweetest, and most charged with electricity we had ever breathed; able to eat chips of dry pemmican three times a day or oftener, and ready to swear that Lucullus had never known our joys of the table; sleeping every night a sleep as sound as that which knows no waking, and rising before dawn at the half-breed's cry of "lève, lève," bright as larks and hungry as hawks. Every man of our party declared that he never had had such a trip before. And yet this year we preferred to go — by rail!

One sees little anywhere from a railway carriage; and when the country is pretty much of a dead level, covered with a uniform net of thick grass, green or russet, according to the time of year, the view from the window soon ceases to interest, and no one regrets that he misses two or three hundred miles of it during the night . . . . It is no use blinding our eyes to the truth that the sun of the North-West has its spots. Ten or eleven years ago I could get few to believe that there was anything good there. Two years ago few would allow that there was anything bad. Bye-and-bye we shall understand that like every other country it is a mixture of good and bad. We may be thankful for enormous areas of good land, vast fertile plains that shall be an inheritance for our children's children . . . . The North-West has many disadvantages. The one that will be felt most sorely for many a day was the

Calgary, circa 1883-1884 *Glenbow-Alberta Institute, Calgary, Alberta*

"boom" of two years ago that unsettled values and demoralized the people. Floods, grasshoppers, early frosts, monopolies, Chameleon land-policy have been small evils compared to the drinking and gambling, the rage for speculating engendered, the laying out of imaginary town-sites and consequent cheating by wholesale, the formation of wild-cat companies, the fictitious values everywhere, the attempt to build up towns before there was any country to support them, and all the other evils connected with the craze to get money suddenly, to get it without working and to get it at other people's expense. Gray-haired men seemed to lose not only their old-fashioned honesty, but their senses. They talked as if half a million or a million of people could be poured into a country by one road in a year of five or six months, and a wilderness of stubborn glebe turned into the garden of the Lord by affixing names to town-sites and locating railway stations. The settlement of the North-West will take time, and the more time it takes the better for the country in the end. Intending settlers, too, had better make up their minds to endure hardships or stay at home, for they need not expect to escape what has been, and always will be, the fate of the average immigrant. The

men who made Ontario and the other older Provinces were of the right stuff. So are the men who have settled in Minnesota and Dakota, hardy Norwegians, Swedes, Welshmen, Canadians who lived at first on potatoes and milk, and were blind to the necessity for completing railways before they had obtained patents for homesteads. The change wrought by them on the appearance of these prairie States in ten years is marvellous. Men of the same stamp have gone into our North-West, and unless we flood the country with a baser sort, like will draw to like. But it cannot be told too plainly that for years to come nobody need go to the North-West but workers and that almost the only workers needed are farmers. There is hardly any honest way of making a living there except by taking it out of the ground . . . .

The Syndicate has therefore at once set men at work to break a few acres at different points all along the line, with the intention of seeding those plots in the spring, and so testing fairly the soil and climate over this enormous area. Not a moment has been lost. This is simply another instance of the ready initiative and the "go" displayed on every occasion, in such startling contrast to the "how not to do it" of

40

Government. The heads give their time and strength to the work, unfettered by the thought of how this or that constituency is to be influenced, or this or that political friend to be rewarded, or by the necessity of having to explain in eloquent speeches innumerable their own virtues, omniscience and economy, and of proving that everybody else is, and always has been, generally lunatic or worse. Governments ought to have advantages over any private company. They can command the services of a higher class of men, even when salaries are moderate, because the positions are presumably more permanent and there is more honour in serving a Government than a company. But when faction reigns, the heads of departments have to attend supremely to their political interests. Every one under them knows that party exigencies are paramount, and as these come in everywhere, paralysis is the result. The people insisted on the construction of the railway being taken out of the hands of the Government; and if no improvement on the party system can be devised, they are likely to call for Syndicates to manage our forests, our Indian department, our education, and everything else that is of importance to the commonwealth as a whole.

III. To Calgarry

After crossing the South Saskatchewan at Medicine Hat, the railroad runs along the watershed between two of its tributaries, the Bow and the Red Deer, the former being some twenty miles to the south of the line, and the latter fifty or sixty to the north. The whole country is beautiful, genuine prairie, great rolling expanses on each side appearing in endless succession — smoothed out at times into absolutely level plains, or broken here and there by knolls or "buttes." Sometimes the horizon is five or six miles distant, and an Indian on horseback galloping at full speed looks like part of the prairie or a speck crawling slowly along its surface. Elsewhere gentle undulations, swelling to a height of fifty or perhaps a hundred feet, contract the horizon, and the track runs in a long valley with easy slopes .... and on the prairie the purple flowering sage, golden rod, marigolds, asters and roses, the characteristic flora in August of Manitoba and eastern Assiniboia, though not with the same wealth of vegetation. The herbage is short and scant, and its withered appearance makes it resemble Ontario autumn pastures, rather than the never failing green of the fertile belt. The grey is relieved by occasional green hay meadows that were shallow ponds in spring, and by deeper lakelets, on the shores of which snipe walk about unconcernedly. Geese are flying slowly round, offering tempting chances to sportsmen, and duck are everywhere. The prairie is seamed by the clearly defined narrow trails of the countless herds of buffalo that once made this country their home. They travelled in single files, heading for water by the most direct road. In days of old, for thus we now speak of yesterday, the buffalo was everything to the Indian — staff of life, clothing, leather and lumber, but to-day scattered skeletons and skulls, bleached white by successive fires, are the only traces of those countless thousands that once blackened the prairie, except the numerous trails which look more like ancient furrows than anything else. The shores and bottoms of dried up ponds sometimes show a white crust of alkali instead of the usual rank marsh grass. To the traveller intent on present necessities, and to the ordinary settler, no sight is more hateful, though the amount of alkali in the soil is only what good farmers consider beneficial to put on their land in the shape of lime or phosphates. This view of the case does not strike a man who is tired and thirsty. When, after travelling for days without seeing a sign of running water, or for hours without a drink of any kind, he comes to a lake or "slew" and finds it bitter, he feels disposed to send the whole country to Coventry. The medicinal effect of even the drinkable water tempts sound teetotallers to carry flasks; but unless "permits" have been secured they know that these may be confiscated by the Mounted Police, and their owners heavily fined . . . .

Almost every one who knows the condition of things in the North-West admits that prohibition there has been, and is a blessing. Contractors, ranchmen, Indian agents, missionaries and settlers unite in generally supporting the law, railway contractors in particular, for their men's sake and their work's sake. I met employers of labour who had been successively on the great Transcontinental railways, and they concurred in saying that nowhere had such good work been done as on the Canadian Pacific, and simply because the men could not get whiskey for love or money. There had been little or no sickness and little or no grumbling, in spite of the bad water and other inconveniences incident to life in the wilderness. Thousands of navvies, many of them lawless, and spendthrifts by nature and habit, accustomed to the free use of revolver and bowie knife, artists in the matter of profane swearing, had lived quiet, sober, industrious, cleanly lives, because whiskey and the usual pests that whiskey allures to

camps had been kept out of the country. Not far from those masterful men in masses, at different points along the line, were thousands of Indians, the men with rifles, the women with little sense of shame, and to maintain order, a nominal police usually kept pretty busy by horse thieves and routine duty. The elements of Pandemonium have been in our North-West for the last two or three years, with one exception. Given whiskey, we should have had on a portentous scale murder, villainy, demoralization, all ending in Indian wars costing millions in money and far more in national disgrace. Indian policy requires a prohibitory law in the North-West . . . .

In spite of the Mounted Police, some whiskey, always of the strongest kind, is smuggled in, and there is a general cry that the permit system is abused. But one duly licensed house would import more in a week than all that filters through in a year by these ways; and as long as there is only one railway into the heart of the country, the law can be fairly carried out, for a system of search is comparatively easy. Of course human ingenuity, especially when stimulated by hope of gain and the delight of evading the police, is full of resource and is certain to keep up a never-ending still beginning contest. The evening before we arrived at Maple Creek station, the officer had noticed a clerical-looking gentleman with suspiciously large valise stepping off the train. Politely insisting on the privilege of examination, spotless shirts appeared on the top and good literature in abundance, with other articles that every gentleman is supposed to require; but underneath, a fine assortment of bottles of brandy that had escaped the notice of the sergeant, who had examined on the train. Alas for the pedlar, who had perhaps invested his all in the venture! He had run the gauntlet of inspection safely inside the car, only to fall a victim to a monster, outside. His brandy, every bottle of which he had hoped to convert into half a dozen, was there and then spilled on the ground, in a convenient spot where some Crees, lounging about the station, could at any rate kneel down and smell it; and he himself, unable to pay the hundred dollar fine, was sent by the next train to the gaol or guard-room at Regina.[14] But he will have his revenge when he is a free man again. He will write letters — probably anonymous — to the press, denouncing the tyranny of the Mounted Police, and the respectable class who believe what is in the papers will feel vaguely that something must be wrong, for "where there's smoke there must be fire" you know. The fraternity of thieves ranges from the pickpocket to the millionaire who steals a railway; and from the smuggler who is happy if he can

42

sneak away from the train with a flask in his pocket, to the importer who hides in crates of crockery-ware enough to poison a village.

To pioneers who have fought with trees and stumps for a lifetime to make a cleared farm, or who have had to plough along the sides of steep hills, boundless expanses of open prairie present a picture of beauty of which they never tire. Others are apt to find the monotony oppressive, and the first sight of the hills on the banks of the Bow — twenty miles to the south — was hailed with joy by every one on the car. To us who had not seen a river since we left the Assinaboine, save the south Saskatchewan which we crossed at midnight, nor a tree for hundreds of miles, the sight of the Bow, near the Blackfoot crossing, winding and doubling like an ox-bow, and of its steep banks clothed here and there with cottonwood, was as refreshing as a drink of cold water to a thirsty soul. And the Rocky Mountains, which had for some time hung like banks of cloud on the distant horizon, now came full into view, the main range lifting itself high in air right across our path, a long broken line of everlasting snow crowning the highest peaks. We saw their outlines at noon, and their varied features came out more distinctly every hour, till the sun set behind them, and they shone beautifully in the warm purple light of early evening. Gradually the purple died away into soft blue, and as the moon rose from the encircling horizon behind us, it tinged with its light the straight wall of battlements that rose fifty miles ahead, apparently forbidding further progress westwards. The sight of the Alps as we look to the north from the great plain of Lombardy is not finer. The North-West has no past, but there is a wondrous fascination in its vastness and the promise of the future. And as long as we are within sight of the mountains we can never be without inspiration. To feel their power once is to feel it forever.

To the south of the winding Bow is the chosen country of the ranchmen. These fine fellows are in the saddle from morning to night, and I am glad to think, if we may judge from their own testimonies and the prosperity of their fellows in the much inferior country of Montana to the south, that they are doing well and likely to do better. The Cochrane Ranche Company suffered heavily last winter, thousands of their cattle dying from exposure to the bitter cold and from lack of food, on account of the snow remaining on the ground longer than was expected. The ghastly evidences of half eaten carcases of poor brutes that had been driven from Montana late in the fall and left to perish on the roadsides beyond Calgarry, and in almost every nook and hollow along the upper Bow and its tributaries could be seen by every traveller last summer. The miserable sight made one appreciate the truth that there was in Mr. Bright's lamentation even over the camels that strewed the line of our army's marches in Afghanistan. The other ranchmen when asked for an explanation usually explained those wholesale losses by bad management, or rather an attempt to manage the business from too great a distance. It is unnecessary to go into details, for the company did its best. It has not lost confidence in the country and will learn lessons likely to be remembered in proportion to the costliness of its experience. All the way from the boundary line to Calgarry, the country seems specially suited for stockraising, horses and sheep included. Water and pasture are of the best, and practically exhaustless. In Manitoba the winters are too uniformly severe, and the snow lies too long on the ground without a break. Under the lee of the mountains the Chinook wind licks up the snow and dissolves the ice on the rivers in the most marvellous way. A friend writes last December, "We had it below zero, with bitter winds, for a week. Three days ago it suddenly changed to warm Chinook. The snow disappeared in a few hours and it has been warm ever since. I have to keep the door of my hut open at night and to take off my coat when walking. You may think such changes extreme, but they hurt neither men nor animals. No one is sick here and the horses are fat. There are fortunes to be made out here, and not slowly." . . .

Calgarry was interesting to us as the point where we must leave the railway, and trust to horses or to our feet, and still more interesting as the place where we were to learn whether it was possible to push across in this latitude to the ocean, or whether we would need to flank our own mountains by striking south and taking advantage of the N. P. [Northern Pacific] Railway. It is well known that the main line of the Rockies can be crossed with the greatest ease by any one of a dozen passes; but after crossing in latitude 51°, the traveller finds that he has accomplished little. He is in a sea of mountains. The Columbia River is running to the north, and he knows that at the Big Bend it turns right round and flows to the south. Within this loop — seventy miles wide — which the Columbia makes, is the rugged snow-clad Selkirk range. We had no certain information of a pass across it, or of a trail, even if a veritable pass had been found.[15] And if we did get across those seventy miles, we knew that a third range, called the Columbia or Gold, would rise up before us, and that this also must be crossed before we reached Kamloops, the nearest village in British Columbia to

The Methodist Mission, Morley

Calgarry; and though Mr. W. Moberly had discovered the Eagle Pass across this range eighteen years ago, we had no knowledge as to whether or not there was a trail, and a pass without a trail is little better than a snare to ordinary travellers. Everything, we felt, depended on the information that Mr. Ross, the C.P.R. Engineer,[16] might be able to give us, and in our eagerness to see him, we scarcely looked at the beauties of Calgarry.

IV. The Mission at Morley

We found Mr. Ross at the right time. A courier had just arrived with despatches from Major Rogers, the engineer of the Mountain Division. The Major had pitched his headquarters at the mouth of the Kicking Horse River, so as to have the Kicking Horse section of the railway on one side of him and the Selkirks on the other. Such a central point was also the best for obtaining and distributing supplies. There was an old trail from Washington Territory, and the Columbia River could be utilized for some distance. In surveying, exploring and railway construction in the mountains, almost the first and last question to be considered is how to feed your men, for it is not an army only that may be said to move or march on its stomach. The courier informed us that he had had both difficulty and danger in getting through to Calgarry from the Major's headquarters because of forest fires at different points; that the distance was 170 miles and the trail very bad; and that the fifty miles down the Kicking Horse would probably take us as many days as the 120 miles to the summit, because the farther we advanced the worse the trail became. We now turned to the Major's letter and read it carefully. He reported that there was no doubt of the reality of the pass across the Selkirks, and that two parties had been engaged all summer in making a trail and in preliminary surveys; that the trail was already on the other side of the summit of the Selkirks, and was being made down the banks of the Ille-cille-want at the rate of half a mile a day, and therefore that the longer we delayed the more trail there would be; but, he added, and here came in the most serious part of the letter, there was no trail through the Eagle Pass. A party could not force its way through without Indians to carry their provisions and blankets, and he had no Indians. He therefore advised that we should strike south from Calgarry to the other side of the boundary line, and make for British Columbia by the N. P. Railway and Puget Sound; and then that we should return to Calgarry and Winnipeg by the Eagle, Selkirk and Kicking Horse passes. This could be done by engaging Indians at Kamloops who would bring us through the Eagle Pass, and by that time his trail-makers would be almost down to the mouth of the Ille-cille-want opposite the end of the Eagle Pass. We could make communications with them, and then with him at his headquarters, and he would send us up the Kicking Horse and down the Bow. This was the Major's advice and I for one thought it good. However, we decided not to take it, why, I can hardly say, except that perhaps we had a pardonable ambition to be the first to travel the whole distance from the waters of Lake Superior to the Pacific by our own route. Besides, we had it in our minds that if the Major, in looking for a pass, had forced his way across the Selkirks we ought to be able to do the same. As to the Gold Mountains, we had arranged with Mr. Grahame, the Chief Commissioner of the Hudson's Bay Company at Winnipeg,[17] that unless he heard from us to the contrary on our arrival at Calgarry, he should telegraph his officers in British Columbia to send Indians from Kamloops to meet us at the eastern end of the Eagle Pass. We therefore decided to go ahead, and the courier was sent back to Major Rogers to tell him of our intentions. Our plan involved risks, but Mr. Ross agreed with us that we might take these, all the more that we were not absolutely committed to our proposed plan until we met and cut loose from the Major's headquarters. If, after meeting him at the mouth of the Kicking Horse, we found that a forward movement was impracticable, we could still execute the proposed flank march by going up the Columbia to its source and striking for the nearest station of the N P. Railway. Our course having thus been decided, Mr. Ross informed us that we could take wheels [*i.e.*, wagons] nearly to the summit of the first range, as parties were engaged on construction work all the way up the valley of the Bow; and that on reaching the summit, the engineers there would fit us out with pack-horses, and that we could travel with them down the western slope of the range along the banks of the Kicking Horse River to the Major's cache. Then, providing us with letters of commendation to the engineers, and with two waggons to carry ourselves and luggage and such supplies as we would be least likely to find in the camps along the trail, he sent us forward with all good wishes on the second part of our journey. So expeditiously was all this managed that although we did not see him till after breakfast, we were on the road by noon [Thursday, August 23], and in little more than an hour afterwards we had crossed the Bow in a scow that an enterprising monopolist had established as a ferry-boat. Some people grumble furiously at paying such an extortionate price as 50 cents for crossing a river in a rude scow. They would not have to pay more than 5 cents in Ontario. But we were such base slaves that we paid the full fare, and applauded the ferryman.

Although the mountains apparently tower right above Calgarry, they are really sixty miles distant. Anxious to get through the foot-hills as soon as possible, and into the heart of the snow-crowned peaks, we drove furiously and reached Morley — forty miles on — soon after night-fall, passing on the way several droves of fine looking horses, and the offices of the Cochrane Ranch Company. Morley is the headquarters of the Methodist Mission to the Stony Indians. Rev. John Macdougal — son of our dear old friend who had travelled with us eleven years ago from Winnipeg to Fort Edmonton — was the founder of the mission[18] and is still its head. His brother David, merchant, trader, stockman, farmer and anything else that may be required, was — luckily for us — our companion on the road from Calgarry as far as Morley. Our waggon wheels broke down two or three times, but he coop-

ered them up, with the help of a kettle of boiling water poured over the hubs and spokes, and with stout willow sticks and abundance of rope, so successfully, that they carried us or we carried them to within a few miles of the summit. Every mending made them look less like wheels, but decidedly improved their running capacity . . . .

V. The Mountains of the Bow River

. . . . After leaving Morley we had a glorious day [Friday, August 24] in the mountains. The smoke that had overhung the valley from forest fires was blown away by a breeze and the fires were pretty well extinguished by opportune rain. The mountains rose before us, apparently just at hand, although we knew that Padmore's, where the first range rises abruptly from an elevated valley and closes in on the river so that it is no longer in an open valley but is seen issuing from a gap in the wall of mountains, was more than twenty miles distant. On our way to this "Gap," an opening in the mountains to the left is disclosed. There the Kananaskis runs into the Bow, and up its valley is the Kananaskis Pass. Near Padmore's we are within touch of the Rockies; to our right a huge battlement of rock, then a tower, then a truncated pillar, and then — nearer the road — a huge sloping mass of the most magnificent rock exposures I had ever seen. The stratification is as distinct as the leaves of a book, the dip of the strata being from the west, as if tilted up from the Pacific side. This great mass extends for more than a mile along the roadside, so near that the temptation is very strong to halt and climb up along the steep slope to the summit of the naked limestone. Passing through the gap, just beyond Padmore's — which spot bears the name of a gentleman who settled here, apparently actuated by love of solitude and love of the beautiful combined — the scenery becomes still grander. The gap opens out into parks, through which the river runs calmly, broadening out into almost lake-like expanses. The mountains on each side are streaked with lines of snow. The railway is at an elevation of about 4,500 feet, or as high as the summit of Ben Nevis, and on the south the mountains rise sheer up 7,000 feet more, the last thousand being naked masses of rock. These mountain forms are superb; so varied and clearly defined, and on so gigantic a scale . . . . Single peaks, then a Parnassus, then a group of sisters, and then a serrated range; every possible form, all alike beautiful and on the grandest scale. There are still a few fires in the woods along the base of the mountains, and the air is slightly hazy in consequence; but this helps rather than hinders the effect on the mind of the onlooker. When the weather is perfectly clear, all the mountains within the range of vision seem close at hand, so great is the mass of each. A little haze gives the requisite perspective. When clouds are wreathed round the base or roll midway up, the peaks come out with nothing between them and you, and they seem so near that one fancies he could almost put his hand on them. It seems to me that next summer, when the journey can be made from Winnipeg to the summit of the Rockies in two days, all Canada that can afford the trip will flock up to this valley. Calgarry, Morley, Padmore's, or farther on, Hillsdale in Aylmer Park,[19] or the summit itself would be good centres for sight-seeing, prospecting, geologizing, hunting or fishing. I have not seen the Yo-semite, but to judge from photographs merely, the valley of the Bow should have the preference. As we proceed up the valley the mountains become grander. One, Cascade Mountain, so called from a jet of water that bursts out from its naked stone side half way up and trickles down to its feet, is fully 5,000 feet above the 4,600 that is the elevation of the park at its base. Three-fourths of the 5,000 feet is bare limestone, at one point twisted, elsewhere regularly stratified, and the whole presenting at a distance the appearance of an enormous solid mass of stone. From the Devil's Head, a still higher peak behind, a turbulent stream flows, which we came to know pretty well, for we had to cross it seven times in the course of as many miles. If it be true that a vein of good anthracite coal has been discovered at Cascade Mountain, the realistic settlers will probably change the name to Mount Anthracite. Such a find would be of more value to the country than the recent alleged discovery of gold-bearing quartz, declared to be worth from $70,000 to $150,000 a ton at Castle Mountain, still farther up the valley . . . .

At Hillsdale, twenty-eight miles on this side of the summit, we exchanged our waggons for saddles and pack-horses. At this camp there was a supply store belonging to the railway, and we were furnished with everything that would probably be required to take us as far as the second crossing of the Columbia on the other side of the Selkirks. We grudged sorely having to carry provisions down the Kicking Horse that we would not need till we began to cross the Selkirks, but it was impossible to know in what condition Major Rogers' stores might be, and our commissariat had to be secured. The Hillsdale camp, at the west end of Aylmer park, was the most beautifully situated of any that we had yet seen. It was pitched at the foot of some low aspen and spruce covered hills, looking out to the east on a grassy park of five or six acres on which our teams and the teams of half a dozen other parties, and cattle intended for speedy conversion into beef, were quietly grazing. This park opened out between opposing lines of mountains that rose 4,000 feet above it; double ranges, the lower wooded at the base and then ribbed with long lines of spruce that struggle with the rocks and frost and snow for a bare living, the higher springing from and immediately behind them, great masses of naked limestone contorted by primeval convulsions, polished and worn down by glacial action and atmospheric influences into every conceivable form. Every one of these multitudinous peaks is worthy of a separate description, and would be honoured with it over and over again could it only be transported to the plains — say near Winnipeg. Before long they will probably be photographed to death, and nothing but the art of the photographer can do justice to their infinite richness in detail.

In the forenoon [Sunday, August 26] at Hillsdale we held divine service on a convenient knoll shaded by aspens near the camp. Though brief notice was given, between twenty and thirty assembled, consisting of engineers, doctor, storemen, contractors, prospectors, and one lady — wife of a contractor whose tent was two or three miles distant, and who had come on an errand to the sore, and remained to grace the congregation with her presence. In the afternoon we made a Sabbath day's journey on horseback. After the horrible jolting we had had for three days in our dilapidated waggons over roots, ruts and boulders, through mudholes where we were like to stick and mountain torrents where we were like to be upset, it was delightful to be on a pony's back for an hour or two. At the next camp the engineer was one of "the first eighteen" of the Royal Military College, and we spent the evening with him and his chief, who had accompanied us from Hillsdale. After high tea and a pleasant evening, they made us a first rate bed of fragrant spruce and pine boughs, judiciously placed thatch-wise. A buffalo robe over these, and then three blankets over us enabled us to sleep comfortably, though the water in a pan at the door of the tent was found frozen in the morning [Monday, August 27]. The sharp air had simply the effect of making us ready at six o'clock for a breakfast of porridge and condensed milk, bacon and beans and corn, bread and excellently cooked dried apples, and good coffee. From this part of the valley, Castle Mountain, a magnificent looking turreted rock crowning a great mountain range, rises so boldly that we can study every detail into which the limestone is carved.[20] Those mighty masses look as if they had been piled up by masons, and chiselled and sculptured by artists. In their singular multiplicity and finish of detail the mountains of the Bow River certainly excel the Alps. It is in this part of the valley that the stratified and igneous rocks meet, and of course parties of prospectors and miners are searching for silver and gold. Good specimens have been found, and one or two miners whom we met declared that the district was certain to be another Colorado. But it is so difficult to know whether or not the specimens were carried to the spot in the pockets of speculators, and people have been bitten so often, that average credulity is not so great on the nugget and bonanza business as it once was. "I wouldn't believe it was genuine," remarked one gentleman who had been bitten hard by a salted mine, "if I saw a vein of solid silver jutting out from the rock." However, the Castle Mountain Mining Company and the miners of Silver City are not sceptical.[21] May their "Queen of the Hill" beat Colorado! And so say we all.

VI. The Summit

Five miles on this side of the Summit, the located line for the railway leaves the Bow River, which had guided it thus far into the heart of the Mountains, and up the north side of which we had journeyed from Calgarry. At this point the river, still broad and strong, is seen circling away to the north,[22] while our course was across it and to the west, along an angry stream called Bath Creek. The origin of names all over the West is usually some personal incident. The Bath received its name from an involuntary bath that Major Rogers took on one occasion in its ice-cold waters to the great amusement of subordinates, whose manner of life makes them incapable of sympathizing with anything short of drowning, starvation, or death in some way. After four miles of Bath Creek, we again diverge to the west, up a streamlet called Summit Creek, and by it we soon reach the Summit. Some engineers, dissatisfied with the Kicking Horse Pass, which extends from the Summit down the western slope of the main range of the Rockies to the Columbia, maintain that, by following the Bow or Bath Creek farther up, it would be possible — perhaps by a tunnel or two — to strike the head waters of the Blueberry River, [*i.e.* Blue Verry River] and so reach the Columbia by the well-known Howse Pass. To determine this finally, and because it would be difficult to push work down the Kicking Horse in the winter months, railway construction

ceased a month or two ago near the junction of Bath Creek with the Bow, and a party was sent, under charge of Mr. [James] Hogg, C.E., to make new exploratory surveys in north and north-west directions. If Mr. Hogg succeeds, his line will be very little longer than that now located, which, after reaching the mouth of the Kicking Horse, has to strike thirty miles to the north before crossing the Columbia. It is of no consequence whether this thirty miles of deviation from a straight course is made on the east or the west side of the main range. Should Mr. Hogg fail, the Kicking Horse Pass will be accepted as a *pis aller*.[23] It is not an ideal pass, but it is no worse than it has all along been known to be.

From Hillsdale to Castle Mountain and on to Bath Creek, the scenery becomes more and more striking. Women and children may see it now by rail. A few months ago, only people in the most vigorous health could assert that the beauty was compensation sufficient for the fatigues involved in an expedition. Soon after leaving Calgarry, we met an acquaintance with his face turned homewards. He had gone a few miles up the valley, and had had enough of the Bow. All that he could tell us of the scenery was that "it was terribly dusty." And so it was. The endless teaming for the thousands of men engaged on construction had cut up the rude trail, and it was "terribly dusty;" and forest fires were mingling their dense smoke with the dust. But our luck stood us in good stead. Enough rain had fallen just in advance of us, to lay the dust and put out the fires. Near Castle Mountain we passed through spruce and Banksian pine that had been swept by fire three days previously. Two mules had been burnt, and their drivers were thankful to escape with their lives. The fires were still smouldering, bursting out here and there up the sides of the mountains; and the effects of the smoke curling up and round the bare cliffs by day, and of the fires burning brightly at night, were superb. As we neared Bath Creek the smoke increased so much that we could not see distinctly to any distance. To the south, a magnificent range extends from Hillsdale in a succession of clearly defined peaks; a cone 5,000 feet above the river, with a glacier curtaining one of its sides; next a pyramidal mass, and then a cube with one side scooped out and filled with snow. This we were told, was Mount Lefroy — so called in honour of General Lefroy, who, in his younger days, did good exploratory work in the Rockies. Next to it comes a saddle-shaped summit, and other peaks with crater-like depressions filled with snow and ice; all alike bold and distinctive.[24] To the north, Castle Mountain is the most characteristic. Beyond it, the blackened poles, that the

fires had left as grim monuments of their fury, gave the country a desolate appearance. Where the flames had not reached, all was beautiful; in the valley, dark spruces and the lighter green of scrub pine alternating with the more tender green of the aspen; along the sides of the mountains the forests extending upwards, at first in solid blocks, then more sparsely, and then as solitary trees and shrubs; and, above all, the bare rock towering high in naked majesty.

Before starting up Bath Creek, we completed our packing arrangements. George, whom we had engaged at Hillsdale as packer, had gone ahead to select horses for us out of a number that were grazing here, and to engage Dave, a pal of his, to act as cook. Our dunnage, buffalo robes, blankets, tent, provisions, cooking utensils and axes, were made up into packs, averaging as nearly as possible fifty pounds in weight, and of convenient shape. Three of these were tied firmly by the diamond hitch to the pack-saddle, and the horse was then considered to have a sufficient load for the trail before him. Each of us was mounted, and we had six pack-horses; Calgarry, Buckskin, Steamboat and Methodist being such knowing old stagers that their names may be chronicled. At nightfall we came upon two parties of engineers, in a little grassy park through which a creek was meandering, about half a mile on this side of the Summit, and camped with them. Next morning [Tuesday, August 28] the sun shone brightly through the cloudy atmosphere. Our little park was completely surrounded by spruce whose branches are small and of the same size all the way to the top so that the trees are not unlike monumental pillars. Lofty mountains look down over these; to the south a double-peaked Parnassus, the sides patched and ribbed with snow; and beyond it a range, like Salisbury Crags, Edinburgh, fissured vertically, and ending in a great bluff of rock immediately overhanging the Pass. Right behind them towers a loftier peak, with a glacier down the side; and farther west, successive ridges and peaks. To the south, we see only one mountain. Moving slowly off from camp, we soon reached the little lake from which Summit Creek issues. Here the Pass begins, a level plateau extending about four miles from east to west; a string of three lakes along it[25] mirroring the great mountains, that rise up on both sides for 5,000 feet above the 5,300 feet that is the altitude of the Pass. From Summit Lake runs the creek to the east: Link Lake in the centre neither receives nor, so far as can be seen, sends forth the tiniest rill; and from the third and largest, the Kicking Horse river, a fine stream fifty feet wide at the start, rushes out like a mill-race, and every mile it runs its speed increases. From the side

of the first lake, the mountains to the south open out, tremendous gorges between them filled with snow slides that extend down to the spruce-clothed foot hills. Peaks, bluffs, and ridges, with the intervening gorges, make up a magnificent panorama.

"This," remarked George, who had seen all the transcontinental railways, "will be the boss route for scenery." After returning by the Northern Pacific we agreed with George. The Union and Central Pacific I had seen eleven years before, only to acquiesce in the judgment of the tourist who, looking in vain for the promised sky-kissing summits, returned, convinced that "there were no Rocky Mountains." At Sherman, between eight and nine thousand feet above the sea, the railway winds along a great bare plateau, a few little peaks in the distance more like mole-hills than mountains, alone breaking the monotony of the scene. The Northern Pacific Railway is much better, but the mountains, as a rule, are too far away from the line to be seen distinctly. At every turn the guide-books call upon you to burst into rapture, but the raptures refuse to come. But, up the valley of the Bow, for sixty miles from Padmore's, and down the Kicking Horse, and across the Selkirks, we are all the time within touch of the most striking rock formations I have ever seen. Not so lofty as Mounts Hooker and Brown, farther north, nor as Mounts Baker and Tacoma in Washington Territory, they are so rich in detail and so completely within the range of vision that they constitute a veritable picture-gallery. There is an endless succession of pictures, each a complete whole, that satisfies the eye and mind of the beholder. The beauty of mountains is not only in height and mass. To me, the mountain forms of Mull and Skye in the Western Highlands of Scotland had a fascination that I did not find in the Alps; and I think that poets prefer the Alps to the far loftier Himalayas . . . .

The first day's march down the Kicking Horse was toilsome enough in all conscience. The trail ran straight up and down a succession of precipices so steep that it would have been impossible to sit in the saddle, even if we had cared to burden the horses with our weight. As we toiled after the pack-animals, I felt quite sure of the origin of the river's name. The poor brutes get mired in muskeg, or their feet and legs entangled among slippery, moss-covered boulders, or in a network of fibrous roots, that they are all the time kicking, plunging and sprawling. It seemed to me that a kicking horse would be the one distinct picture graven on the mind of every one who had ever tried to make his way through this valley. I gave the explanation with the utmost confidence to the junior member of our party, but he suggested, as a better, that it was quite evident that no horse would have a kick left in him at the end of the journey. These attempts were as creditable as the guesses of the antiquary or philologists with reference to the derivation of disputed symbols and words, but, unfortunately, an Edie Ochiltree, in the persons of some Stoney Indians whom we met in the evening, blew our theories to the winds. They declared that the origin of the name went back to an experience of that Dr. Hector who accompanied Captain Palliser on his expedition. Hector was a Highland athlete, who could out-walk, out-climb, or out-starve the toughest Indians. Stories of his wonderful feats and medical skill and kind-heartedness are told in the North-West to this day. Well, his horse kicked him when he was in this valley, and the Indians attached sufficient importance to the fact to give the river the name which it has borne since, "the horse-kicking river," — the name which is now known all over the continent in connection with the Kicking Horse Pass. Why the Pass should receive its name from the river that runs down the western slope of the mountains, instead of from the one that runs down the eastern slope, I could not find out. Certainly the Bow deserves the honour. It is the guide of the railway for 120 miles from Calgarry to within sight of the Summit, and a more temptingly open and beautiful roadway, into the very core of a great mountain range, could not be desired; whereas the Kicking Horse is followed for only forty-seven miles, and as to the grades that will be necessary in that section, it is enough to mention that a descent of 2,700 feet is made by the river in its short course. It is impossible to feel very grateful to the Kicking Horse. When rivers get their deserts, the Pass will be called the Bow River Pass; but, until that time comes, we had better continue to call it, under protest, if that will help, the Kicking Horse Pass . . . .(To be continued).

Footnotes

1. W. L. Grant & F. Hamilton, *Principal Grant* (Toronto, 1904), p. 27.

2. *Ibid.*, p. 58.

3. *Ibid.*, p. 220.

4. *The Week*, Toronto, March 6, 1884, "The C.P.R. by the Kicking Horse Pass and the Selkirks. VII." This will be published in the next issue of *Canada: An Historical Magazine.*

5. Sandford Fleming, *England and Canada: a summer tour between Old and New Westminster with historical notes* (Montreal, 1884), pp. 248-249.

6. PAC, G. M. Grant Papers, Vol. 31. Undated letters to his wife, Monday evening [August 20, 1883] from Moosomin.

7. *Ibid.*, Vol. 31, Grant to his wife, Monday morning, August 27, 1883, from Castle Mountain camp.

8. *Ibid.*, Vol. 31, Grant to his wife, Sept. 17, 1883, from Kamloops.

9. *Ibid.*, Vol. 31, Grant to his wife, Saturday, [May 7, 1881], from Toronto. Mrs. Grant seems to have written him so he would have the letter on the morning of their anniversary. They were married May 7, 1867.

10. *Ibid.*, Vol. 30, Charles M. Grant to W. L. Grant, May 24, 1902, from Dundee, Scotland.

11. John Macoun (1832-1920) was appointed Professor of Botany and Geology at Albert College, Belleville, Ontario, in 1868. He had been included in the 1872 journey of Grant and Fleming. Grant here refers to Macoun's western survey for the Canadian government in 1879. In 1882 Macoun became botanist to the Geological Survey of Canada, became Assistant Director of it in 1885 and remained at that post until his death.

12. This is quite correct. Captain John Palliser (1807-1887) spent the years 1857-1860 surveying the Canadian west for the British government. The dry seasons were of course to reappear periodically in the future.

13. Since Sandford Fleming arrived in Halifax from England on August 5, 1883, it has to be assumed that Fleming wrote Grant earlier than August.

14. Prohibition in the North-West Territories dated from 1870, and a new Act in 1873 gave power to any Justice of the Peace to seize and destroy liquor with or without a warrant. It was by virtue of these powers that the North-West Mounted Police exercised the surveillance Grant describes. It can be added that prohibition lasted in the North-West Territories until 1892, when the North-West Territories Assembly, having been given permission so to legislate by Ottawa, introduced licensed bars.

15. As Grant probably knew, Major Rogers had located a pass through the Selkirks in the summer of 1882, after great difficulties. Whether there was a usable trail was the question in Grant's mind.

16. James Ross (1848-1913) was the Engineer in charge of the Mountain Division of the C.P.R. He was later associated with Sir William Mackenzie and President of the Dominion Iron and Steel Company.

17. J. F. Grahame had been stationed in Edmonton when Grant and Fleming were on their 1872 trip and was a familiar friend.

18. Rev. John McDougall (1842-1917) was the son of Rev. George McDougall (1821-1876). The father had been a Methodist missionary in the West since 1860, and he and his son established the Mission at Morley in 1873.

19. Hillsdale is not far from the site of the town of Banff, and Aylmer Park is in the broad sweep of the Bow in the flat valley just west and north of Banff.

20. After 1945 Castle Mountain was renamed, unfortunately I think, for General Dwight Eisenhower. He is alleged to have said, when shown a picture of the splendid mountain named after him, "It's as bald as I am." The top of this long, castellated mountain is 9030 feet.

21. "Silver City", like many mining camps of the kind, has gone. Some ruins are left.

22. The present Banff-Jasper highway follows the main valley of the Bow at this point, and turns northwest away from the Kicking Horse Pass. The headwaters of the Bow River are some 30 miles up this highway, at Bow Lake.

23. Grant is confused here. According to both Sandford Fleming, and Pierre Berton, it was Tom Wilson who, at Rogers' request, had made a hazardous exploratory trip over the Howse Pass in August, 1882. James Hogg was sent in the summer of 1883 to explore the western side of the Selkirks, explored part of it and returned meeting Fleming and Grant a day and half after they had started down the Kicking Horse River. Hogg's description of the western side of the Selkirks gave them a good deal of food for thought. See Grant's article No. VII, in the next issue of this magazine; also, Fleming, *England and Canada*, p. 244, and Pierre Berton, *The Last Spike* (Toronto, 1972), p. 174.

24. These are mainly the mountains that are grouped about Lake Louise and the Valley of the Ten Peaks. Grant did not visit Lake Louise, although it had been discovered by Tom Wilson in the summer of 1882. Presumably there simply was not time.

25. The best known of these lakes is Wapta Lake, just west of the summit.

Reviews

The Barn: A Vanishing Landmark in North America.
Eric Arthur, photographs by Dudley Whitney. Toronto: McClelland and Stewart Ltd. 1972. Pp. 256, illus. $25.00.

In 1964, Eric Arthur's book, *Toronto: No Mean City*, opened our eyes to the architectural riches of a great Canadian urban centre. Where many had seen only a sprawl of church spires, shops, warehouses and Victorian monstrosities, he found beauty, craftsmanship and proud ostentation in the work of builders who were heroically ambitious to re-create the glories of European architecture on the edge of the wilderness. His unfashionable enthusiasms helped to spark a continuing search for comparable architectural treasure, rewarding in both historical associations and visual enjoyment, in other cities across the country.

Now we have the perfect complement to this earlier volume. In their valuable book, *The Barn: A Vanishing Landmark in North America*, Professor Arthur and photographer Dudley Whitney have brought into sharp focus those buildings which have been for all of us, from childhood, signs and symbols of what constitutes rural life and work. We have not looked closely enough at them before because, as storehouses and animal shelters, barns have been too utilitarian and rough in construction to be classed by most people as architecture, a term which carries with it the expectation of formal grandeur and rich ornamentation. However, the authors make us look again and realize that in aesthetic and historical terms, barns mean more to us than we have thought. The superb collection of photographs by Whitney, so deftly composed and, thanks to the publishers, so often in full colour, remind us how imposing a barn may be. They make us recall farms that we have glimpsed from a highway or explored at leisure during a hike along a country lane. Barns dominate these recollections, barns soaring above the trees or rambling along the roadside, red-planked with swelling gambrel roofs or grey and sharp-gabled like great ships riding the swell of the fields, moored to their silos. Barns are certainly big in the eye and in the imagination, and they often display an impressive harmony of simple proportions deriving from the taste of builders who were disciplined, even at this geographical and social distance, in the principles of the classical tradition. Thus the barn can have its own kind of grandeur, bearing comparison with so-called higher forms of architecture.

Barns have their own wealth of ornament too. This is not decorative carving or painting of stone and wood in traditional patterns, although something of this is seen occasionally in very charming forms. Primarily, it is a more natural and instinctive decoration of contrasting textures and materials, rough-hewn timbers, boulders set in thick mortar, patterns of light and shade on artfully placed boards, thatch and shingles, together with many other visible traces of the handcraft process itself. These things are picked out in loving detail by the sharp eye of the photographer, confirming our impression that here is architecture, and as the text rightfully insists, sometimes great architecture.

Professor Arthur is full of respect for these anonymous barn builders of Canada and the United States, and he discusses their work on several different levels, historical, technical, aesthetic, and geographical, but what may impress most are intimations of something deeper. This appears in his frequent comparisons, specific or implied, with church architecture. The frame of the barn is often designed like a high nave with side aisles; the soaring interiors evoke cathedral spaces; the silos remind us of bell towers; the great round or centralized barns resemble medieval baptisteries, and the community effort required to raise the barn was like community involvement in the erection of Gothic cathedrals. This leads us to think of the barn at the highest level in almost religious terms, and after all, it was the centre of ancient methods of cultivation which became a kind of ritual, linking man spiritually as well as physically with his environment. Consequently, in a mechanized world, we are filled with nostalgia for the sense of harmony between man, God, and nature expressed by the varied forms of the barn and summarized by an inscription photographed by Whitney. It is on a stone lintel from a barn raised in Ontario in 1863. "When your barn is well filled, all snug and secure / Be thankful to God and remember the poor."

Paul Walton
McMaster University

Beaverbrook. A. J. P. Taylor. London: Hamish Hamilton [Toronto: Thomas Nelson]. 1972. Pp. xvii, 712, illus. $13.50.

"People do not read to be bored" was Lord Beaverbrook's dictum. And no one need fear that it will be broken when A.J.P. Taylor, the master and scourge of the historical profession, takes as his subject one of the most colourful characters of the twentieth century. Like everything else Taylor writes, his *Beaverbrook* is first-rate entertainment as well as good history.

Here again is the famous staccato style, the energetic verbs, snap judgments and Tolstoyan twists of irony. Men delude themselves into thinking that they can impose their mastery on events, find themselves pushed in all kinds of unexpected directions or acting for no very clear motive and try later to justify their erratic course by forcing it into some coherent literary framework. Taylor has always enjoyed deflating these pretensions and even The Lord himself occasionally comes in for the familiar treatment.

And yet, this is not quite vintage Taylor. His hallmark has always been a robust refusal to take people at their own valuation. But this time he is dealing with the man he loved "more than any human being I have ever met." On one occasion, he recalls, Beaverbrook so inspired him that "he saved my intellectual life. I went home, sat down at my typewriter and did not pause until my book was finished . . . . The full debt of gratitude I shall never repay." If such fulsome praise makes the reader squirm uneasily, it also explains how Taylor can present in such a favourable light Beaverbrook's empire crusade, his political manoeuvrings and the way he ran his newspapers. Much is explained also as a function of his irrepressible sense of fun: "The drawing pin on the chair gave him pleasure as a boy, and its political equivalent gave him pleasure as a man. If he saw two naked wires he could not resist putting them together, whatever the resulting explosion." This is a refreshing perspective on "Robin Badfellow", but not entirely convincing. There is too much testimony, brilliantly summed up in the "Working for the Beaver" sequence in "Beyond the Fringe", to his irritability, autocracy and abrupt changes.

As a companion, Beaverbrook must have been delightful, and he was certainly generous to his many friends, from R. B. Bennett and Rudyard Kipling to Aneurin Bevan; but he must have been hell to work for. How many below the rank of cabinet minister or editor joined in the shouts of laughter that surrounded him? Who dared even smile when he sternly told the students of the University of New Brunswick (of which he was the great benefactor and life chancellor by provincial statute since his virtually single-handed appointment of the president): "Alan Taylor has come a long way to lecture to you, so listen very attentively." Despite Taylor's most stimulating efforts, it is impossible to see Beaverbrook as a genuine radical. Unorthodox, yes; a burr under the saddle, certainly; but not one who basically disagreed with the Conservatives' view of politics and society.

Beaverbrook's adventures in England were made possible by the fortune he accumulated in Canada, largely before his thirty-first birthday in 1910. He had a sure financial touch and promotional skills perhaps unrivalled in the business history of this country. Taylor, no economic historian, tells the exciting tale of Max Aitken's rise from son of the manse to Montreal millionaire in just forty-two pages and gives us a fascinating glimpse of our neglected gilded age. Here, surely, is a story as dramatic as the building of the C.P.R. awaiting the investigation of some enterprising historian.

Lord Beaverbrook always considered himself a Canadian, took a keen interest in the affairs of his native land and kept announcing his intention to return. A Canadian reading this account is assailed by two conflicting emotions. The first is regret that he did not remain, the second relief that he left. He might have livened up the long grey years of Mackenzie King — yes, and of Meighen, Bennett, Manion and Bracken too. But reason intrudes on these fanciful thoughts. English society, like a great oak, was large and complex enough to contain him. He served it well in the Second World War and gave it a healthy shake in the late afternoon torpor of the interwar years. But he might have broken the Canadian sapling.

Neville Thompson
McMaster University

Booze: The Impact of Whisky on the Prairie West. James H. Gray. Toronto: Macmillan of Canada Ltd. 1972. Pp. xiv, 243. $7.95.

When Canadians opened the West, liquor was there and lots of it. It had been bad enough when the drinkers were a scattering of Indians and traders, but when railway workers poured in and the C.P.R. began to burp and hiccough its way across the prairies, respectable citizens felt that something had to be done. That something was prohibition.

James Gray's *Booze* examines the prohibition movement and prohibition in the prairie provinces from the 1870's to the 1920's. It begins with the awesome level of frontier drunkeness that was part of the reason for prohibition and ends with an account of the prohibition movement. Gray makes a strong case for the effectiveness of prohibition, despite many evasions of the law. He also discusses those distillers and brewers, notably the Bronfmans, who made fortunes on dark prairie nights. The fact that many of them were Jews added to the racism that had always been a component of prohibitionism. But they were assisted by a legion of Christian politicians and civil servants about whom Gray raises many pertinent questions.

As always, Gray has a sharp eye for the ordinary man and the local scene. His anecdotes about drunken N.W.M.P. constables and about chains dragged by rum runners' cars to smother pursuers in dust make the best of what was already fascinating material. The accounts of prairie towns with smells of stables in the rain and the clamour of sweating men in crowded bars are vivid. *Booze* is a brilliant sound and light show.

Occasionally, it is more than that with hints of what lay below the surface of prohibition. There are sudden insights but no sense of their significance and they vanish as suddenly as they appeared. Though entertaining, *Booze* shows only a limited understanding of its subject.

Briefly, Gray interprets prohibition as essentially a religious movement and he sees its rise as a response to heavy drinking. Its decline is attributed largely to local conditions in the prairie provinces. There is some value to this interpretation but much of it is superficial.

While it is true that some churches were closely identified with prohibition, the closeness had little to do with theology. Those churches were middle-class institutions and they adopted prohibition because non-drinking was then part of a middle-class value system. That value system, which also included church attendance and regular work habits, was not accepted by the working class. Thus the attempt to impose prohibition on it. It was assumed that an end to drinking would also end a myriad of other problems such as poverty, crime, industrial inefficiency and neglect of religion.

Canada's middle class also felt threatened socially and politically by the growth of a working class. If the middle class could force its values on the whole country through legislation, it would at the same time reassure itself that it was still the dominant class. Gray notes that the impetus for prohibition was related to the growth of towns, and this is one of his flashes of insight that should have been pursued. It was a product of town life because it was in the towns that class confronted class and that social problems were most apparent.

There were many other aspects to prohibition. For example, it was related to imperialism and the missionary effort of the time. All were justified by the belief that the dominant value systems of Europe and America were superior to any others and that there was both a right and an obligation to impose them on the rest of the world.

The movement was advancing in much of the western world throughout the nineteenth century. It declined in much of the western world shortly after World War One. Just as the rise of prohibition cannot be understood purely in terms of conditions on the prairies, so neither can the decline. The reasons for that decline have yet to receive adequate study. One reason, possibly, is that World War One cooled much of our optimism about reforming the world. In this respect, the decline of prohibition may have been related to political isolationism in Canada and the United States.

Because it relies so heavily on anecdotes and local records, *Booze* fails to convey much of the significance of prohibition. It is far from being an adequate history of prohibition in the Canadian west. But it is first rate reporting by an engaging and gifted writer. It should be an important source book for the history yet to be written and it will certainly enrich any shelf of Canadiana.

Graeme Decarie
Loyola College

The Dictionary of Canadian Biography, Vol. X, 1871-80. Edited by Marc La Terreur. Toronto: University of Toronto Press. 1972. Pp. xxx, 823. $20.00.

Volume X, which includes biographies of prominent Canadians who died from 1871 to 1880, is the third volume of the *Dictionary of Canadian Biography* to make its appearance and the first section of the work to deal with the nineteenth century. The previous volumes, I and II, had dealt with the period 1000 to 1740; now the editors will work both forward and backward, with alternate volumes, until the entire period up to 1880 is complete, before moving on toward the present. In the past, similar national biographical collections usually have been organized alphabetically, rather than by date of death. This new arrangement means that people who flourished at the same time will appear in one volume, or closely related volumes, and not be spread over the entire range of the *Dictionary*. Thus each volume will present a picture of a period by itself and therefore will be of more immediate use than if the volumes were arranged purely alphabetically. For comparison, the French dictionary of biography, which was begun in 1933, has only reached the letter D and no historical period will be available completely for many years.

The *Dictionary of Canadian Biography* was established under a bequest of James Nicholson, a Toronto businessman who wished to provide Canada with a multi-volume dictionary of national biography, equivalent to those available in Great Britain and the United States. Thanks to the efforts of the first editor, the late Professor George Brown of Toronto, it is appearing in both official languages under the auspices of the presses of Toronto and Laval Universities. A grant from the Centennial Commission enabled the editors to begin work on the nineteenth century and thus paved the way for this latest volume. Nicholson particularly desired that individuals be included who made contributions to all walks of life, so there is not that emphasis on political, religious and literary figures which is apparent in so many other collections. Also, all aspects of an individual's career are dealt with in each article, not just such activities as politics, which are so often overemphasized in a biography. Finally, the *Dictionary* includes not just the great, about whom it is relatively easy to find information, but also secondary figures whose contributions to Canada have been obscured by the passage of time.

Naturally, the politicians still play a major role in the volume and the decade of the 1870's saw the passing of many of the major political figures of Canadian history. For Nova Scotia there is Joseph Howe, who led the battles for Responsible Government and against Confederation, and his Tory opponent, William Johnston, whose abilities here receive due credit for the first time. From Quebec are to be found Louis-Joseph Papineau, who dominated the Rebellion of 1837, Tory Sir George-Étienne Cartier, Sir John A. Macdonald's closest associate at the time of Confederation, and English Reformer Luther H. Holton. From Ontario there are William Henry Draper, Tory leader before Responsible Government and later Chief Justice, Reformer George Brown, one of the most important of the Fathers of Confederation, John S. Macdonald, first premier of the new province and Ogle R. Gowan, founder of the Orange Order. Colonial governors are also represented: Sir James Douglas, father of British Columbia and Sir Francis Bond Head, the traveller and author whose ineptitudes sparked the

Rebellion in Upper Canada. In other areas of endeavour there are ecclesiastics, such as Anglican Bishops Edward Field of Newfoundland and Benjamin Cronyn of London, painters Paul Kane and Cornelius Krieghoff, and author Philippe-Joseph Aubert de Gaspé. Sir William Logan, the geologist, is also present and such business figures as William Molson, John Torrance and John Young.

In general the balance is a good one, though a few of the biographies appear to be a bit longer than their subjects merited, and there is something of a tendency to try and equalize representation from the various regions of Canada. But in opening a new era, the first study of the nineteenth century, the editors have generally done a fine job. The volume, with its extensive bibliography and biographical index, will not only provide a basic reference for public and private libraries, but also interesting delving in itself for readers who enjoy Canadian history.

Frederick H. Armstrong
University of Western Ontario

Mike: The Memoirs of the Right Honourable Lester B. Pearson. Vol. I, 1897-1948. Lester B. Pearson. Toronto: University of Toronto Press. 1972. Pp. x, 301. $12.50.

Among Canadian political figures, the art of writing memoirs is not highly developed. In their years of retirement Tupper and Borden tried their hands at it, but the results were not memorable. The first volume of L. B. Pearson's memoirs is in a different category, not because great secrets are revealed — for they are not — but because in terse and sprightly prose he has described most effectively the circumstances which shaped his development and his years as a civil servant. The man who takes shape in these pages gives substance to the public figure with whom perforce most of us had to be content; the honesty of his self-portrait enables us in retrospect to appreciate and to sympathize with the virtues and the failings of the man who became a distinguished minister of external affairs and a greater prime minister than contemporary pundits and critics judged him to be.

Mike volume one, recounts Mr. Pearson's life from his birth in 1897 in a Methodist parsonage to his appointment in 1948 as Minister for External Affairs. His mother, long disappointed that he had not become a clergyman, then commented: "I am glad you have at last become a Minister, if only a second-class one."

This unconcern for worldly rank and honour was only one of the qualities instilled in Mr. Pearson by his family and his church. To be able to laugh at oneself, "to be kind and understanding to people I passed on the way up, since I would no doubt meet them again on the way down," integrity, and above all a genuine concern for the moral implications of all actions were unquestioned elements in the atmosphere of the Pearson home. So, too, in these days of frustrated search for our national identity, it is well to be reminded that for the Pearsons this was not an issue. Sturdy Canadianism blended imperceptibly with an identification with things British, an attitude exemplified in Mr. Pearson's later policies and which he was able to transcend on the domestic front, because for him justice and equity for Canadians were more important than cultural traditions and preferences. From his family Mr. Pearson also derived a sense of status, and intellectual concern, that encouraged and enabled him to proceed to university. In his case, roads lay open from the university into academic life, the emerging career civil service and the Liberal party. In English-speaking Canada, the parsonage and the college have been, as Mr. Pearson's career indicates, important agents in the formation of that "meritocracy" which John Strachan and Egerton Ryerson thought indispensable to our national development.

Mr. Pearson's experiences in college, as a long-suffering and yet cheerful soldier, and at Oxford in the early twenties fostered and deepened his awareness of Canadian parochialism and propelled him imperceptibly toward the foreign service. One of an unusually able group of aspiring diplomats in External Affairs after 1928, he developed rapidly, not least in his judgment of men and events. His assessment of King and Bennett, two antipathetic characters, who in their turn aroused violent antipathies in others, is discerning and sympathetic. Mr. Bennett's "storms were rough, but they were usually of short duration and often cleared the air." "I do not recall that Mr. King ever stormed," rather where "Mr. Bennett would burst into flames, Mr. King would smoulder .... He would reproach himself in your presence for expecting too much of a young officer." Bennett's political career is epitomized by his exchange with Howard Ferguson just before the 1935 election. "How is the campaign going, R.B.? Fine, Fergy, we have them licked." From the outset too, Mr. Pearson agreed with the thrust of Mr. King's policy. "The reason for his strategy (in dealing with the British) became clearer to me later, even though I never could approve or even wholly under-

stand some of his tactics which seemed over-subtle to the point of mystification". "In a very real sense," he continued, "Mr. King was a 'Canada First' isolationist, notwithstanding all his emotional speeches on the mother country . . . and his equally emotional reflections on the brotherhood of all men . . . . "

As a career diplomat in London, Washington, and Ottawa, Mr. Pearson was himself a believer in "Canada First," but his perception of what that entailed steadily broadened from a rather shaky support for appeasement, to an increasingly sophisticated conception of the meaning of collective security for Canada. He learned that "there is a great deal to be said for 'velvet glove over the iron hand' diplomacy, but nothing for the 'iron glove over the velvet hand,' " that although American officials often flew about like confused bees "bearing with them both the menace of sting and the promise of honey," differences with them could be settled "in a frank and outspoken manner." Many Americans and others, were, as Eisenhower claimed to be, "idealistic as hell," but they often applied their ideals naively. By 1945, Mr. Pearson was convinced that Canada's safety lay in the acceptance of international responsibilities and that it must live with its status as a power strong enough to be necessary to the great powers but "not important enough to be accepted" as one of them. Canada's "continental policies," he was sure, "would be not only vitally important, but increasingly complicated and difficult . . . ," an accurate forecast indeed.

Thinking as he did, Mr. Pearson naturally if reluctantly moved into politics when Mr. St. Laurent, who shared his views, became Mr. King's heir apparent. "I recall so well Mr. King's remark on hearing this. 'Now, St. Laurent, we're going to have to get him elected.' " This was almost a shock to Mr. Pearson, in itself a foretaste of his subsequent political detachment and of his political difficulties. But, the shrewd, humble, conciliatory and imaginative man who is depicted in this volume was not swamped or demeaned by politics. To read his account of the subsequent turbulent years should be a happy and illuminating experience for students of politics and for every Canadian who seeks to comprehend the legacy of those years.

G. S. French,
Victoria University

Samuel de Champlain, Father of New France. Samuel Eliot Morison. Boston, Toronto: Little, Brown and Company. 1972. Pp. 227, appendices, bibliography. $11.50.

Morison's *Champlain* is a popular biography based on extensive use of primary sources. The style is informal and the narrative is laced with modern comparisons and personal references: for example, sexual promiscuity among the Indian youth of Champlain's day is compared with sexual behaviour in a 1972 college dorm; Champlain's seamanship, as was Columbus' in Morison's earlier book, is tested against Morison's own expertise and experience along the same routes. Morison's language frequently verges on the colloquial. To eliminate an opponent is, in Morison's parlance, to "rub him out." In general, then, the volume is pleasingly written, attractively published, and generously illustrated. Some fifty reproductions of maps and drawings by Champlain and recent photographs of the historical places involved grace the narrative; an accurate map of early seventeenth-century French North America is the only omission of consequence. A thirty-page appendix, Champlain's treatise on seamanship, may also interest some readers.

The reader is given a detailed account of Champlain's explorations of the New England coast to 1607, his penetration of the St. Lawrence system to 1616, and his careful nurturing of Quebec until his death in 1635. His qualities of leadership, courage, piety, and humanity towards the Indians, as well as the barrenness of his private life clearly emerge. In the face of the mother country's disinterest in New France, Morison shows that Champlain's energy was largely responsible for making New France a going concern. Yet the French Crown gave him no honours or distinctions, and only his death spared him from learning that he had been replaced as leader at Quebec and that his successor had been given a higher title.

In spite of its merit, Morison's *Champlain* will be a disappointment to those who have read Morris Bishop's biography: *Champlain, The Life of Fortitude.* Morison offers no reinterpretation of Champlain, and he has not utilized recent studies which might have permitted him to do so. Is Morison correct, for example, in attributing France's humanitarian Indian policy to Champlain's personal example and influence? French policy was at least partly the result of the fur trade frontier in which the Indian was an economic ally of the European, rather than an economic enemy as he was in the English frontier of settlement. To take another exam-ple, recent secondary literature strongly disputes Morison's judgment that New France's seigneurial system "was the most successful feudal land scheme in all North America."

In summary, Morison's *Champlain* is an enjoyable popular biography. Readers can appreciate its style, brevity and illustrations. But for understanding Champlain, Morison's volume is no better and in some ways less valuable than Bishop's biography.

G. N. Emery
University of Western Ontario

Sculpture of the Eskimo. George Swinton. Toronto: McClelland and Stewart Ltd. 1972. Pp. 255, illus. $18.50.

The problem facing anyone interested in Eskimo sculpture has been to try and find it, for comparative purposes, in substantial collections. If this situation has begun to change, we are in debt to George Swinton who has been an enthusiast ("one who is possessed") on behalf of Inuit art.

His first book, *Eskimo Sculpture*, published by McClelland and Stewart in 1965 was a smaller compendium which described in general terms the varieties of Inuit sculpture. In 1970 he mounted a retrospective showing of sculpture by Tiktak of Rankin Inlet and published a catalogue of the show, *Tiktak — Sculptor from Rankin Inlet, N. W. T.*, (Winnipeg: University of Manitoba Press). In 1972 a second show appeared, "Eskimo Fantastic Art," and with it a catalogue also. He was the initial force behind the "Sculpture/Inuit: Masterworks of the Canadian Arctic" which opened in Vancouver and, after two years on world tour, will be returning to Ottawa in the spring of 1973. In addition he has been the lodestone of many public and private collections. "Art always is an assertion," Swinton writes, "an affirmation, an act of faith. As such it always changes and, as long as it is able to change, it lives." (p. 143) Such are the convictions which animate George Swinton's interest in Eskimo art.

Sculpture of the Eskimo is composed of two catalogues with approximately forty pages of text. In describing his purpose the author states: "All that I have done in this book is to record visually the relationships of styles and subject matters within the better-known areas of the Arctic as an initial step in that very important field of Arctic research." (p. 139) Consequently, the contents of the first catalogue, reminiscent of André Malraux in that it attempts to be, in the words of the author, "a museum without walls", were chosen to show the variety of Inuit sculpture. The photographs have been cropped to uniform size (with the result that some which were blown up appear blurred) and twenty-eight of them appear, one to a page, freely without the visual competition of margin or captions. Another thirty-four also appear singly on pages with margins and credits. If we look at this section of approximately one hundred photographs as a kind of engaging kaleidoscope, it is a great deal of fun. Anyone who is familiar with the German Expressionist tradition will feel at home with many of these sculptures because of the associative imagery they provide.

Swinton's museum without walls is, however, a museum without a sense of scale and without any subject titles or descriptions. The result is a visual pun in which the viewer puts away measuring rod and suspends all questions. The author's defence is that "the labels of the commercial, the official, and the academic worlds . . . obscure the true relevance of the Eskimos' art and predispose us to certain aesthetic judgements. These judgements too frequently prevent deeper appreciation of the art form." (p. 13) On the contrary, instead of burying the few particulars that we have, should we not continue to assemble them in order to preserve the scant information available and to make it more widely known? While many descriptions may not be authoritative, it is possible to indicate where there are areas of doubt; and this is surely preferable to abandoning all titles in order to play it safe. It helps to know, for example, if the sculpture is about a man or a woman; about a spirit or an abstraction; about a family of animals, or different aspects of one animal, and so on.

The question of scale has to do with assumed relationships of size. If a photo of a sculpture is page size, then it would be helpful to indicate that illustration 142 is at a scale of 1:1; or that illustration 140 has been reduced by one-half, whereas illustration 125 has been enlarged to twice its actual size. The reader then would have a way of knowing what he is really looking at — the ability to envision the sculpture in the sculptor's perspective — without holding a tape measure in hand.

The author also missed the opportunity to add to the identification of Eskimo sculpture by indicating when new identifications have been made. For example, illustration 122 is attributed to Annie Niviaxie, yet it was described in the catalogue of Sculpture/Inuit as

unknown. How has this identification been made? Similarly, in *Eskimo Sculpture* (1965) the artist on page 165 is described as Erkoolik; but in illustration 25 of *Sculpture of the Eskimo* (1972) the sculptor is listed as his brother Tikeayak. It would be helpful to have an explanation of the change.

It is in the second half of the book, "Catalogue of Artist by Area" that it is possible to see, to really see, something of the range of Inuit sculpture. In this second catalogue, the format of horizontal line with captions above and photographs underneath is a unifying device which, although it suggests a textbook treatment, is not at all distracting. Rather, it serves to hold the photographs together, and the changing scale makes it possible to comprehend them more easily and with greater interest. With approximately six hundred photos on one hundred pages representing more than twenty areas, one can appreciate the effort involved in this assemblage which brings together many sculptures previously presented in Mr. Swinton's first book, *Eskimo Art*, in the catalogue of Tiktak's work, in the later catalogue *Eskimo Fantastic Art*, in the catalogue *Sculpture/Inuit* and many more. It is to be hoped that catalogues may now be gathered together of individual areas and artists as well, and we are indebted to George Swinton for showing the way.

The text, entitled "The Sananguaq-Art Concept," is intended to provide a conceptual basis for Inuit art. In it, Swinton argues that "one point is certain: while the contemporary *inuit* art forms are not stylistically related to the past, the strong connections the *inuit* have with the past reappear today as vivid echoes which have been blended together with completely new reflections of the changed environment." (p. 110) Eskimo sculpture, in other words, is an intimation of Inuit culture, just as it is an imitation of reality. Swinton's definition of *sananguaq* (which also appears in the foreword to the *Sculpture/Inuit* catalogue) is "a likeness that is made or carved," a "model, imitation or likeness." He notes, however, that the artists themselves "have not yet determined what the criteria of excellence are, but rely largely on the sananguaq-art notion: art as reality, art as truth, art as effective communication." (p. 130) This critical void leaves ample room for Swinton to take the Sananguaq concept onto a high level of abstraction, without having laid down the particulars which might define it. Continuing in this vein in his essay on the subject of "Aesthetics-Inuit vs. Kablunait" he writes: "the true differences between *inuit* and Western aesthetics can only be found in evaluations and attitudes and not in styles. Eskimo aesthetics appear to be non-linear, process-and-content oriented; Western aesthetics predominantly linear, product-and-form oriented." (p. 133) Whether the author is making an assumption here, or drawing a conclusion, he is moving in one direction, a wide circle. And he finally comes full circle when he asserts that ". . . art has to be apprehended through the senses and not through the intellect; intelligent 'understanding' of a work of art does not lead to liking it, and, vice versa, one does not need to like a work in order to understand it . . . ." (p. 133) If the mind and the senses do not always reinforce each other, that does not mean that they cannot do so. Moreover, it is surely the task of the humanist, the scholar, the artist to put them as much in touch with each other as possible. The questionable dialogue which follows, as Swinton tries to imagine how an Eskimo, an art critic and a non-art-collector would react to three different sculptures, is a sad burlesque, a partiche which evades. Finally, in his essay "The New Art Form" the author concludes that in Eskimo art

> The work is contained in its form. That which is form is the work as it is experienced. It does not prove anything, but it convinces. It is a cyclical argument: the form of a work of art is its content; the content of a work of art resides in its form; the subject matter is given form and becomes content; the subject matter can never be the content; when it is, then the work is not art. The subject matter can be analyzed; the content and the form can only be experienced. (p. 142)

Fortunately, a "museum without walls" is its own justification.

Undoubtedly there are problems involved in presenting a general visual history of Inuit art for a nonspecialist audience, while at the same time trying to lay the guidelines for aesthetic theory, particularly one which is derived from the subtleties of Inuit linguistics. But after reading this text, one feels that George Swinton is rather like a notary feverishly looking for a birth certificate, whose, he is not sure — perhaps his own. We are all in his debt for the visual record he has assembled, but his search for a theory of Inuit art is defensive and premature, albeit completely well-intentioned.

It is to be hoped that ever-increasing collections, research and published catalogues will add to our knowledge of Inuit art because it takes many years for the academic world to formulate the questions relevant to any new form. It is absolutely necessary, therefore, to keep track of the information we do have, to add conscientiously to the written word so that a coherent record will be available to those artists and scholars who in subsequent times will search out the larger framework, and provide an understanding, of Inuit consciousness.

In the meantime one can agree with the author that ". . . through his art, the Eskimo became capable of overcoming the very weariness and irrelevance that seems to have overtaken much of the Western art impulse." (p. 25)

Helen Cappadocia
Hamilton

Contributors

About the Contributors

COLONEL C. P. STACEY, who teaches history at the University of Toronto, served as Historical Officer at Canadian Military Headquarters, London, England 1940-45, becoming Director of the Canadian Army's Historical Section after the war, and Official Historian of the Army for the Second World War. In addition to his official writings his books include *Canada and the British Army 1846-1871*, and *Quebec, 1759: The Siege and the Battle.*

JAN KUPP teaches history at the University of Victoria, Victoria, B.C.

LOIS DARROCH MILANI's articles and poems have appeared in *Canadian Forum*, *Ontario History* and major Canadian newspapers. A former secondary school teacher she now runs her own publishing house, Ampersand Press. *Robert Gourlay, Gadfly* is a first book.

PETER WAITE has written two books, *The Life and Times of Confederation, 1864-1867* and *Canada, 1870-1880: Arduous Destiny*, as well as a number of articles. He teaches at Dalhousie University, Halifax.